# 50 things you really need to know

# BRILLIANTLY BEHAVED TODDLER

Lorraine Thomas

Quercus

# Contents

# Introduction

Becoming a mum or a dad is a life-changing
experience. It's the most rewarding and challenging
job you'll ever do in your life, and definitely the
most important, because your input now will affect
your toddler's ongoing approach to life.

Children come with no instructions and while
it's possible to parent perfectly well without help
from other people, sometimes it's possible to feel stuck or unsure about
how best to deal with toddlers, who can present a wide-ranging set
of challenges! So we've put together the best up-to-date advice and
practical tips to help you handle your toddler's tantrums, nurture their
wellbeing and have fun.

As a parent you hold your child's hand for a short time, but their heart
forever. This means that your influence is enormous – everything you say
and do is being absorbed by your little one as a demonstration of how
to do things, from getting dressed in a particular order to dealing with
arguments successfully. At the same time, your toddler is also beginning
to assert his independence for the first time, and will behave in ways that
you might find very challenging.

That's where this book comes in. It will help you see the world through
your toddler's eyes and understand what makes him behave in the
way that he does, which will go a long way towards helping you deal
empathically with him in any situation. We suggest lots of simple,
practical tools to help you deal positively with difficult behaviour, many
of which can solve the trickiest of problems in just a few minutes a day.

If you have ever felt that your toddler, not you, controls family life, this
book will put you back in the driving seat and enable you to enjoy being
the kind of parent you want to be.

Lorraine Thomas

# ① Parent taming

Being a parent is the most important job you'll ever do – and the most challenging. Every parent knows just how stressful it can be when your toddler screams and shouts to get his own way and you end up doing the same. His behaviour – and yours – is, however, perfectly normal.

## Parents have tantrums too

It's normal for a toddler to 'throw a wobbly' and flex his muscles. It's a natural part of his growing up and your development as a parent. What's interesting is that the majority of mums and dads have tantrums at one time or another too. In the parenting workshops that I regularly run, around nine out of ten parents admit to shouting at their children, saying things they later regret and feeling guilty. Most say that they lose their temper when their toddler is throwing a tantrum in public or in the evenings when they find it most difficult to stay calm themselves. This is because when we're feeling tired and under pressure, we have far less patience and little things can bring out the worst in us, meaning that small incidents can escalate into major wars.

> Yelling. Throwing toys. Stamping. That's me, not them! #guiltymum

This demonstrates how the key to having a brilliantly behaved toddler is having a brilliantly behaved parent. You are and always will be your child's most powerful role model and every day is an opportunity for you to make a real difference in his life. But remember too that you're only human. So when you're setting expectations around standards of

Parenting sometimes feels like mountaineering – it's exhausting, relentless, and occasionally you'll stumble. So reach out for help from your fellow climbers; their support can make all the difference.

behaviour, make sure you don't set the bar so high that you make it easy for yourself to fail, which will then lead to you feeling guilty. There's no such thing as the perfect child – or parent!

## Holding up a mirror

Your behaviour is the most important factor in teaching your toddler how to behave. He holds up a mirror to you. Take a close look into it and you'll see that both the things you love about your child's behaviour and the things you find most challenging have their roots in you. So while you can't wave a magic wand over your child and change his behaviour, you can begin today to make changes in the way that you behave and in the way that you respond to him. Changing your behaviour will bring about positive changes in your toddler's behaviour too. If you are a calm and positive parent who rises to challenges, you're likely to have a child who behaves like that too.

# You're in charge

You probably feel that your toddler knows just what to say or do to make you lose your cool. He knows which buttons to press – you may be determined not to react in a particular way, but somehow he seems to know how to make you act like that despite your good intentions. It's at times like this that parents sense that their toddler is in the driving seat and has somehow gained control. Your toddler throws a tantrum and you react to it, without having time to think about what's happening in the heat of the moment. What's happening here is that you have fallen into the trap of acting your toddler's age, instead of your own, and effectively there are now two toddlers having a tantrum!

It is easy to be calm, in control and positive when things are going well in family life, but it's much harder when you are tired or stressed or your child is being particularly challenging. The first step to being calmer is to believe you can do it. If you think you can, you will. If you think you can't – you'll be absolutely right about that too. It isn't easy. It takes real strength, energy and commitment to decide to stay calm in stressful situations. Like lots of things about being a parent, this skill isn't learned in an instant; you may have to work at it on a daily basis. But the more you practise, the easier it becomes.

# Lower the volume

It's natural for parents to raise their voices and shout to be heard. The TV may be on, the washing machine spinning, and a bunch of noisy toys may be in play. As your child gets louder and louder, you may find that you do too, in an effort to be heard over all the noise. But raising your voice and shouting raises your stress levels and often doesn't work, because as you increase your volume, your child might raise his too. If you get into the habit of using tone instead of volume, you'll be much more effective. Instead of shouting, get down to your child's level and look him in the eye. Lower the tone of your voice and sound decisive. He'll soon learn to use tone instead of volume too.

# Top tips for parenting toddlers

- Believe in yourself. If you believe you can handle your toddler's tantrums well, you will.
- Get out. Plan at least one fun activity that will take you away from home.
- Go with your gut instinct. Watch out for the warning signs before a full-blown tantrum occurs, and create a diversion.
- Don't rush in. Commit to be calm, take a deep breath and count to three. Focus on your breathing as you decide how you want to deal with his tantrum.
- Take control of the situation.
- Act like a parent, not a child. You can't change your toddler's behaviour by shouting, but you can by setting a good example.
- When you look at your toddler, see the child you love. See a child learning to be independent – not being deliberately difficult.
- Stop giving attention to behaviour you want to discourage. Behaviour that gets attention, gets repeated.
- Don't take anything he does or says personally. This is about him learning to be independent. It's not about you.
- Don't frown – smile! It has been scientifically proven to make you feel better.

## Condensed idea
**Keep calm and act your age, not your toddler's!**

# 2  The dos and don'ts of discipline

Good, positive discipline is a vital part of your toddler's life and it's important to have it there from the word go. If the 'terrible twos' is a dress rehearsal for the teenage years, then getting into good habits now will benefit you and your child for years to come.

## The meaning of discipline

Discipline is a very positive concept. While the positive word 'discipline' can sometimes be confused with the negative word 'punishment', they are in fact very different. Discipline is about providing a clear and practical framework within which your toddler can grow and develop.

The word discipline comes from the Latin word meaning 'teaching' and, as a parent, you are your child's most important teacher. In these crucial early years your toddler is totally dependent on you, learning everything about life from what you say and what you do. You start off with a blank slate and it's up to you to decide what life lessons you want your little disciple to learn and the best way to teach her. This will include how to behave, how to develop relationships with other people and how to be a valuable member of your family and the world. It's a huge and exciting responsibility.

## You are the managing director

You'll already be doing a lot of things well when it comes to discipline and setting boundaries, but it's essential to build on these strengths. Mums and dads are good at giving themselves a hard time about what they don't do and rarely step back to acknowledge what they achieve on a daily (even hourly basis). As a parent, you're the managing director of the most important company in the world – your family. You make great decisions about all kinds of issues – strategy, logistics, budgets, personnel issues, health, safety – and crisis management. You probably take all that for granted because you don't have time to stop and think. But it's important to acknowledge what

> Thought we agreed on everything to do with discipline. Forget same page – not even in same book! #mum&dad

you achieve, as it will give you perspective. Often we focus on the bits of family life that aren't quite working and forget all the bits that are. Discipline is really about strategy – about having a plan. You have all the skills, experience and personal qualities you need to make it a success. You just need to stand back a little, focus on your strengths and take the time to decide what you want for your family.

Think of discipline as a game of chess: if you have a strategy, you stand a better chance of winning.

# Two parents, one message

Before you had your son or daughter, you and your partner probably thought that you agreed on everything to do with being a parent. But now your toddler is here, you may well be finding that actually you have very different ideas on a day-to-day level. Discipline is often an area where parents have different beliefs about what they want to achieve

## Start with the basics

Knowing the basic rules in discipline is the first step to achieving a successful relationship with your toddler.

**Do...**
- think: discipline = framework, security and nurturing
- be positive about discipline. If you are, your toddler will be too
- believe that discipline is a creative tool to energize family life
- say what you mean – and mean what you say
- give attention to behaviour you want to encourage
- remember your ABC – Always Be Consistent
- go with your gut instinct – you're the expert on your toddler

**Don't...**
- think: discipline = punishment, rules and nagging
- be negative about discipline. If you are, you toddler will be too
- regard discipline as something that restricts family life
- make idle threats and false promises. They don't work
- give attention to behaviour you want to discourage
- keep moving the goalposts
- be influenced by others and what they do

and the best ways to go about achieving it. So if this is your experience, be reassured that it is totally normal. You may feel very unsure about the 'rules' here. Children don't arrive with an instruction booklet – you have to learn on the job. Every phase of your child's life will bring with it new experiences and challenges to handle, and you will develop your own parenting style as you go along. Your style is likely to be different from your partner's, and in some areas, that's fine. However, if you want to have a brilliantly behaved toddler who feels secure as she develops, it's essential that you and your partner have a consistent approach to discipline. Remember that you're a team and you need to find a way to work together, so be prepared to negotiate and compromise. If you don't, your child won't know whether she is coming or going and can't really be held responsible for acting inconsistently herself. If you and your partner live apart, make sure you're still following the same approach to discipline; if your toddler spends time in different homes getting different messages, she will become anxious and confused.

## Be positive about discipline

If you're positive about discipline, your toddler will grow up being positive too. When you are developing your ideas on discipline for your toddler – and finding out what works and what doesn't – you're being a very positive parent. Throughout this process, you'll be making important decisions. In this book, we'll be offering you lots of useful, practical and relevant tools for use in all sorts of everyday family situations. But you're the expert – so what's really important is that you look at what's available and decide for yourself which ones are right for you and your toddler. Put them in your toolbox, adapt them to suit you, and make them work for you.

## Condensed idea
### Every toddler needs positive discipline to learn how to behave

# 3 Setting boundaries

Setting boundaries is an essential part of healthy family discipline, and whether we are adults or children we all need them. They give our lives structure and order and they also show your child that you care about her and what she is doing.

## From toddler to teenager

Setting effective boundaries and sticking to them in the face of adversity is a challenge every parent has to face, at every stage of their child's development. Your little daughter may be stamping her feet because she doesn't want you to switch off the TV or go to bed. But it won't be long – and the years will rush past like an express train – before you have a teenager who is arguing about turning off her computer or refusing to go to bed before you do. If you set the precedent by putting boundaries in place now, you'll find it easier to set new ones as your child gets older.

## Don't let the toddler set the rules

Keeping to your boundaries is where the rubber really hits the road. All children buck against rules to some extent and may push your boundaries to the limit. This is a normal part of growing up and learning to be independent, but it may also represent one of your biggest challenges. Being a parent is tough. We all want our children to grow up with the confidence to have a strong sense of self and to be independent, but when a toddler demonstrates those very qualities, we can find them really difficult to cope with. So as you are deciding when to put your boundary plan into action, choose a time that's good for you. In order to make this work, you need to be feeling as positive and energized as

# How to set boundaries that work

The following checklist will help you set clear boundaries and make them work:

- Focus on one boundary at a time. Decide what you want to make your priority: early mornings, bedtimes, TV, sleep and so on. Don't try to set new boundaries for everything at once.
- Be specific about what you want to achieve. Instead of saying 'I want Jamila to be in bed earlier than she is at the moment', for example, say 'I want Jamila to be in bed by 6.30 p.m.'
- Focus on the benefits of making it work – for you, your toddler and the rest of the family.
- Be clear and use positive language with your toddler about what you want her to do. Tell her and show her.
- Make sure your partner and other significant adults are sending the same message.
- Take a reality check. Step into your toddler's shoes and make sure that what you're expecting of her is realistic.
- Believe you can make each boundary work.

possible, so only attempt to address boundary issues when you've got time and energy; not, for instance, after a stressful day at work.

Even with the best will in the world, it's hard to be calm and stand your ground when your toddler is screaming and you're feeling tired and stressed. In these situations it can be tempting to ignore some naughty behaviour 'just this once'. But while that may solve the problem in the short-term, you'll be making your life much harder in the long-term.

# Your role and behaviour

There are four important things to remember when setting boundaries:
parents need to be realistic; detached; and consistent – and children
always respond to attention. You can use a toddler's love of attention
constructively here by giving your child specific praise for keeping the
boundary. If you tell her exactly what it is that she is doing well, she will
carry on doing it. Motivate her by using praise, stickers or star charts,
and don't give her attention for behaviour you want to discourage. Be
realistic by remembering that your toddler is a very little person and she
has to work hard at this; acknowledge what she may or may not be able
to do. Lastly, don't take anything she does as a comment on yourself –
it's about her learning to be independent, not about you. Be consistent
in implementing any boundary and make sure that your child knows
exactly what's expected and what the rules are. For instance, instead of
saying 'Don't get out of bed', say: 'Now I have tucked you in, I want you
to stay in bed.' Make the rules as clear as possible; rather than saying

something vague such as 'You've seen enough TV now – it's time to turn if off', say: 'We always turn off the TV after watching Teletubbies.' Steer away from using negative rules, as these only encourage bad behaviour (by suggesting what your toddler can do to provoke a reaction). For instance, rather than saying 'Don't throw your food', say: 'Try hard to keep your food on your spoon.' If you can maintain a new boundary for at least seven days (often much less), you will notice a significant difference in your toddler's behaviour.

## Using 'time out'

Don't be surprised if your toddler occasionally forgets where the boundaries are and steps over them. 'Time out' is a simple, practical and effective tool you can use in these situations. Identify a safe location with no distractions (so she will be bored enough to think about what just happened). A bean bag in the hall or the bottom step of the staircase work well, but don't ever refer to these as the 'naughty' chair or step. Ask your toddler to sit there for several minutes (make this appropriate to her age – perhaps three minutes for a three-year-old) and explain that this is so that both of you have time to think about what's happened. You're creating a space to reflect on how you want to respond to your child's behaviour, from a position of feeling calm and in control. Most importantly of all, remember that the time it's most important to love your child is the very time she makes it most difficult to do so.

> Someone's moved the bedtime boundary. Gone AWOL. Sure I put it in a safe place yesterday. #familyopenallhours

## Condensed idea
### Strong boundaries help family life run more smoothly

# 4 Tuning into tantrums

**You are the expert on your toddler and once you begin to tune in to what makes your child tick, you'll begin to understand what makes him explode. Then you can look out for the warning signs and develop your own tailor-made strategies to deal with challenging moments.**

## Step into your toddler's trainers

Take a look at the world through your toddler's eyes for a few minutes now and then, and you'll begin to understand something of what's going through his mind. Unlike you, your toddler lives only in the moment – he really doesn't consider the past or future. All that's important to him is what's happening here and now. That's why when he wants something, he wants it immediately – and he will let you know it. He is in an exciting new world with lots of exploring to do and he needs your help to do this. At the same time, there are certain basic things he needs to keep him happy, just as you do.

## What makes you both happy?

Think about the times that your toddler seems to be in his happiest state and what you do to bring that about. Being a parent is an art, not a science, but there are definite things that you can do to nurture your child's contentment. Your toddler is likely to be at his happiest, most content and fun when he is energized, has been fed, is engaged in an activity he enjoys and is getting your attention for behaving well. Toddlers are really quite easy to please. Just like you, he functions best when he has had a good sleep, has a full tummy, is doing something he's interested in and is getting encouragement.

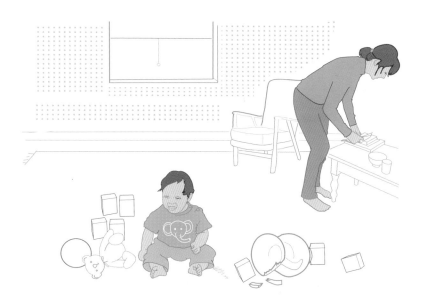

# Watch out for the warning signs

When your toddler is not happy, you'll soon sense it. Go with your intuition; it's likely that you're already picking up some of the warning signs – usually that he's becoming tired, bored, hungry or frustrated. As soon as you spot signs of one of these 'big four', take action to stop a tiny turn from becoming a full-blown tantrum. Your toddler will be sending you a message loud and clear. If he's hungry, feed him; if he's getting tired, let him sleep or move to a less demanding activity. If he's frustrated, try to work out why, and help him. If he's bored, help him to move to a new activity. When you sense that trouble is brewing but there's no identifiable reason, try distracting him with a fun activity; he'll usually forget what he wanted to make a fuss about.

# Parent-induced tantrums

It's not surprising that some toddlers throw their toys out of the pushchair if a parent has decided to pop out to the shops before feeding them. If your toddler is tired and hungry, a tantrum is likely to occur. So

# The power of ignorance

Attention is the key to understanding what makes your toddler tick and shaping his behaviour in the way that you want. Behaviour that gets attention gets repeated, so be sure only to give your attention fully to behaviour that you would like to see again. Your toddler is desperate for your attention – ideally, positive attention. If you can, try to catch him 'red-handed' doing something good. Make sure you use specific descriptive praise when he is doing something you want him to do (describe what you see so that he knows exactly what it is you like). Your toddler is then much more likely to repeat that behaviour.

However, if a toddler can't get positive attention, negative attention will do (any attention is better than no attention). If he is doing something you don't want him to do, you might imagine the best way to deal with it is to tell him to stop. But in all likelihood, you'll find that he does it again. Unintentionally your behaviour will have produced the opposite effect to the one you want, as you're sending your toddler the message that if he keeps doing what he's doing, he'll keep getting your attention. That's what he wants, so, according to his logic, it makes sense to keep doing it. You've lost, he's won.

Toddlers really don't like being ignored. If it is safe and possible, give your toddler no attention for behaviour you want to discourage. Learn when to let things go without comment. Your toddler will soon get the message that behaving in this way doesn't achieve what he wants.

be careful that you don't create stressful situations through your own actions. If there are certain things you do that commonly result in a tantrum, think about how you might do them differently and pay special attention to what your toddler is trying to tell you. Even if you are both feeling stressed, listen to what your toddler is saying and take practical steps to help him get to a calmer place. If you reduce his stress levels, you will be reducing yours too. Build regular meals and routines into

> **Toddler time bomb ticking…**
> **#dadtakingcover**

his day, and give him a mixture of times to be active and times to rest and recharge his batteries. Also, remember that it works both ways – you will find your toddler most demanding when you are tired and hungry. So make sure you look after yourself too.

Keep reminding yourself that life can be frustrating for a toddler. He wants to be independent and to show you that he can be, but at the same time he can't perform physical tasks as quickly as he wants to. He also has enthusiastic but limited means of communication, so tune in to what your toddler is trying to tell you and learn to take the word 'no' in your stride. Be realistic in your expectations, too: toddlers get bored very easily as they have a very limited attention span (a two-year-old has an attention span of just two minutes and a four-year-old just four minutes). This one of the key reasons for toddler explosions. Eventually your toddler will learn to keep himself occupied, but at the moment that's your job. Above all, remember that in every family there are always lots of things going on and a toddler won't always get it right.

## Condensed idea
### Once you tune in to what makes your toddler tick and explode, you'll be a master tantrum tamer

# (5) Toddlers aren't perfect

There's no such thing as the perfect toddler – or perfect parent – and that's as it should be, because otherwise family life would be very dull. In fact, much of a toddler's most extreme and challenging behaviour is totally 'normal' and experienced by most parents.

## Don't compare toddlers

You only have to take a look around the park, or nursery, or supermarket to see that what one parent considers normal and tolerable toddler behaviour is very different from another's. You might see young children behaving in a way that you would find totally unacceptable in your little one – but their parents aren't batting an eyelid. If you think about it, you'll probably find that, in fact, what you accept as normal and tolerable varies from day to day. Just like your toddler, you probably have good days and bad days. If you're feeling positive, you rise serenely to the challenges of toddler behaviour, but if you're stressed, you probably don't. Toddlers have very strong willpower and if your toddler sees a chink in your armour, she'll make the most of it.

Love your toddler for the person she is. She'll be different from her siblings and any of your friends' children. Enjoy her individuality and try not to judge her behaviour against the behaviour of other toddlers.

## Be positive about your skills

Parents of toddlers can find themselves feeling negative about their parenting skills. This will probably be because your expectations of your toddler's behaviour – and your own – are unrealistic. It's normal for mums and dads to perceive themselves as failing because they struggle with their toddler's behaviour; parenting a toddler is one of the toughest jobs you'll ever do, but luckily you'll get daily practice. Recognize the enormity of what you have already achieved and don't underestimate the challenge of the mountain you have yet to climb.

# Me, me, me!

It's normal for your toddler to want your attention and object to being ignored, because she believes that she is the most important person in the universe. If a toddler wants something, she wants it immediately. Toddlers do very little thinking and certainly don't pause to weigh up the pros and cons. They aren't interested in negotiation, because they just want action. That's why your toddler is likely to stamp her feet and shout to get what she wants. Listening to reason is not a toddler strength and at the same time her sheer determination to be independent might be quite daunting. Your toddler may refuse to be fed or dressed or be helped into her pushchair – even if she is too young to do it herself.

Toddlers are born active. Forget going to the gym – you have your very own personal trainer. They're also naturally messy and it's what they do well (I've never met a tidy toddler and don't expect to!). So don't expect perfectly tidy rooms, but do encourage your toddler to tidy up her room with you, perhaps talking about her clothes and toys as you do so.

Your toddler needs your constant attention. Always remember that she has little concept of danger and even the most sensible toddler will sometimes act on impulse. Her behaviour will be affected by all sorts of things, from the kind of mood you are in today to any slight changes in her routine. She'll demonstrate extremes of behaviour whenever she is very happy, upset, worried or stressed. And, yes, she will change her mind all the time – you're not going mad when you think this. She really does love bananas, red socks and toothbrushes one moment and hate them the next.

> She's an angel with dad and devil with me. What's going wrong?
> #confusedmum

## Better behaved with others

During my parenting workshops, I've discovered that around three out of four mums of toddlers say their confidence has taken a 'significant knock'. One of the key reasons given for this is that a mum might find her toddler difficult to control, but then be astonished by how well she behaves in the company of other adults. It's a fact of life – just ask any other parent – that your toddler will behave for other people in a way that she refuses to do for you. Some mums say that although they struggle with their toddler, she is very well behaved with her dad. Of course some dads say the very opposite is true. So what's the reason for that? Attention. For a toddler, getting her parent's attention – in the way that works for that parent – is her sole purpose. Understand that and accept it, and don't give yourself a hard time. It's not you; it's a strategy she is using to get what she wants: your full attention.

# Real parents talking

At the parenting academy where I teach, we carried out a survey to find out how parents of toddlers really feel about their abilities and responses as parents. The findings gave us a good insight into 'normal' family life with a toddler in tow. And the good news is – you're not alone if parenting a toddler makes you feel stressed. This is the period where you can really begin to understand what the actor Ed Asner meant when he said that 'Parenthood is part joy, part guerrilla warfare.' Our survey revealed that:

- 9/10 parents find their toddler's behaviour 'very stressful'.
- 8/10 parents say they often feel their toddler is 'in control instead of them'.
- 9/10 parents confess to acting their toddler's age at least once a week.
- 9/10 parents say they have doubts about their parenting skills.
- 8/10 parents find their toddler's challenging behaviour in public the most stressful aspect of being a mum or dad.
- 9/10 parents admit to shouting and then feeling guilty.
- Toddler behaviour patterns that parents of 2–4 year olds found most stressful were temper outbursts, arguing and resisting bed.

## Condensed idea
Your toddler is a unique little character, so be sure to enjoy every moment of this stage, because it won't last long

# 6 Talk and be heard

**One of the biggest complaints parents voice is that their toddler just doesn't listen to them. It's true that toddlers aren't natural listeners, but they hear much more than you think they do. By putting some practical strategies in place, you'll soon begin to notice a significant difference.**

## Listen well

Your toddler's word bank will usually begin to explode at around 18–24 months. She'll jump from saying a few words to having a vocabulary of over a thousand words by the time she's three. It's an exciting time for both of you as you can start to have real conversations. The challenge for you will be to get a word in edgeways!

The best way to help your toddler develop great listening skills is for you to demonstrate them yourself. All parents know how often they say 'I'm listening' when really they're too busy doing 100 other things to hear what's being said. You might have good intentions, but find that often there's simply too much going on. This can be a real challenge, especially when your toddler loves chatting non-stop and expects your full attention. The key is to only say you are listening when you really are. Your toddler will know when you're not listening, and if you say that you are, she's much more likely to kick up a fuss. Try to listen more: the more listening you do each day, the fewer tantrums she'll have.

However, always be realistic; don't attempt the impossible. You can't listen intently to everything your toddler says, but you can listen properly sometimes. The quality of your listening will affect how she listens to other people, and the more you listen to her, the more she will learn to listen to you. So whenever you can, switch off your mobile or laptop, turn off the TV, and appreciate that the two of you are together, at this special time in her childhood. Her viewpoint is unique and you could actually get a very interesting view of the world from her. So get down to her level and listen completely. Look at her when she is speaking (if you shout from another room, she will too) and make eye contact as you speak. Encourage her to do the same with you.

## What to say and how to say it

- Give toddlers simple, clear instructions, such as 'Put the toys in this box' rather than 'Put your toys away'. Suggest they 'Take it in turns to kick the ball' instead of asking them to 'Play nicely'.
- Do not phrase directions as questions. For instance, say 'It's time for bed' rather than 'Are you ready for bed?' (which invites the answer: 'No!').
- Introduce choice where possible. For instance, 'Do you want to get into your pushchair like Cinderella or Buzz Lightyear?'
- Acknowledge your toddler's feelings (positive and negative); make sure you don't deny them. If she's upset when leaving friends, say 'I know you are disappointed about leaving the party', not 'Stop moaning, you've had a good time.'
- Set your toddler a challenge. Say 'See if you can get your shoes on before I can' or 'See if you can get into your pyjamas before I count to 10.'
- Use 'when' and 'then'. For instance, 'When you have cleaned your teeth, then we can have a story' or 'When you have put on your coat, then we can go to the swings.'

# Notice how you say it

The way that you speak to your toddler and the body language you use will be as important – if not more important – as the words you choose to say. Stick to some simple rules and she'll be much more likely to listen. Be positive, clear, confident and definite; show her that you mean business. Lower your tone and your volume and look her in the eye; this will encourage your toddler to listen more effectively. Don't keep repeating yourself, because that is stressful and nothing happens (and your toddler will learn to do the same thing). Ask once in your usual voice, then once in your firm voice, and if she still ignores you, take appropriate action. If your toddler ignores you when you ask her to share a ball with a friend, for instance, tell her what you are going to do: 'I am going to roll the ball to Katy, because I want you both to take turns. When Katy has rolled it back to me, I am going to roll it back to you. We can have lots of fun together.' Then take the ball and do it. Your toddler may have a tantrum when you do this, but if you give your attention to Katy rather than to your daughter, your reluctant toddler will soon want to play with you both.

# Play listening games

There are lots of fun ways to develop your toddler's listening skills too, such as playing 'ear-spy' with her. Choose a sound you want her to listen out for – a car, laughter, a dog barking – and see how quickly she can hear it. Or try introducing the 'listening spoon'. This is particularly useful if you have more than one child. Have fun letting your toddler draw a face on a wooden spoon, then

> She's got perfect hearing for the word 'chocolate'. But for 'bedtime'? Deaf! #allears

explain that if anyone wants to speak they have to hold the listening spoon. She will begin to learn not to interrupt you and to wait until you have finished speaking. She will get excited about the moment when you pass her the spoon and will begin to understand that she can only speak when she has the spoon in her hand.

Enjoy spending time listening to stories and music with your toddler. Ask her simple questions to find out if she is listening and encourage her to ask you a question. This will teach her to tune in to what she is hearing without visual clues. Make up a story with her, using her favourite toys and her friends as the characters. You can start the story, then encourage your child to make up the next part, taking it in turns as you go. This is a great way for a toddler to learn to listen to you carefully, so that her part of the story makes sense. Praise your toddler for listening well and make sure you are specific so that she'll do it again. Have a special 'listening time' or day and give her a 'well done!' sticker each time she shows listening skills. She can give them to you too – but only if you are really listening!

## Condensed idea
### Your toddler will listen to you if you learn to listen to her

# 7  Food fights

**Mealtimes can be stressful and minor food battles can easily escalate into full-blown wars. You dish up his food feeling like Mary Poppins, but clear away feeling more like Cruella de Vil. Cut your stress levels by taking control and start playing the meal game by your rules, not his.**

## Toddler mealtimes are messy!

Toddlers find food as exciting as paint or playdough, so when you're dishing up breakfast or dinner, expect some mess. Be realistic about your expectations before you start serving up a meal, because a toddler doesn't have your table manners – and he won't for a long time. He is learning to be independent and he wants to do so much himself, even if his little hands and mouth aren't up to the job yet. He's learning a whole new set of skills, so when you see him struggling and ending up with food all round his mouth and all over the table, stay calm and try to see it from his point of view. A toddler's attempt to eat spaghetti by himself is like an adult trying to eat spaghetti using chopsticks. An almost impossible and incredibly messy task! So relax and enjoy this time with him and try not to fret about the mess he's creating. If you're constantly jumping up to wipe him or the table down, you'll both feel tense. When your kitchen looks like a crime scene, remember that your chores will always be there, but your children won't. Before you know it, they'll be out every night and you'll be wishing that they were back sucking up that spaghetti and making you smile with their earnest perseverance.

> Take cover...it's tea time! Turns out that food can fly. #themumchef

# Toddlers are fussy

Many toddlers are picky eaters. It goes with the territory but it's one of the main reasons that many parents find food times particularly difficult. If you're not careful, mealtimes can become an opportunity for power struggles between parent and child. What your toddler eats – or not – is one of the few things he can control; he's likely to make the most of this by making demands designed to show who's boss. Don't enter into a battle of wills when your toddler is odds-on favourite to win; he's very unlikely to share your spinach pie. Work with his tastes, within the bounds of healthy eating, and don't try to force him to eat anything or mealtimes will become stressful for both of you. A toddler will soon learn that if he doesn't eat, he will be hungry. Keep your sanity and get your toddler to develop healthy eating habits with a few practical strategies. Motivate him to eat by getting him involved in meal preparation, such as cutting up bananas or cheese. Let him help arrange the food on his plate, perhaps making it into a smiley face with carrot or spaghetti hair. When he goes along with your wishes, make sure you give him lots of praise.

If you throw a tantrum to get what you want, your child will too. Toddlers love to say 'No' because it's a great way of getting your attention. The harder you try to make your child eat, the more determined he'll be to refuse. Avoid negative attention by praising him for what he *has* eaten. And as always, don't take anything your child says or does personally.

## Top tips for stress-free meals

- Create a TV-free time before eating.
- Encourage your toddler to help you with the meal. He'll be much more likely to eat food he's helped to prepare.
- Serve up small plates of food that he can finish, but have extra food on hand so he can come back for more. Cut the food up into manageable bitesize pieces and, if he's reluctant, set him a realistic goal of taking just one or two bites.
- Don't get angry if food isn't eaten. Praise him for eating well.
- Be relaxed about table manners. It's normal for a toddler to use his hands instead of knives, forks and spoons.
- Get him into the habit of regarding healthy foods as 'treats' rather than assuming he won't like them and will need to be bribed with unhealthy 'treats' to eat them.
- Be creative. Toddler food needs to look inviting.
- If your toddler does not like a variety of foods, it is safe to give him a repetitive diet as long as it is nutritionally adequate.
- Keep preparation simple. It's hard to keep calm when he turns his nose up at a meal that's taken you hours to prepare.
- Invite a toddler friend who likes to eat to come for tea – your little one is very likely to follow his friend's example.

He's not doing this just to make your life as stressful as possible. He's learning to be independent, and meals are a great place to demonstrate his growing awareness of himself and his likes and dislikes. It's normal for toddlers to have unpredictable eating habits. He will be inconsistent, eating really well one day and then perhaps eating only a small amount the next. He may love carrots one day – and hate them the next. He may want to do everything himself today but expect you to do it all for him tomorrow. Children are as changeable as the weather. A toddler's lifestyle lends itself to snacking, not sitting down to meals. Toddlers are constantly on the go, so always have some healthy snacks available (remember that his behaviour will deteriorate when he's hungry).

## Mealtimes are family times

If you want your toddler to learn about sit-down meals and how special family mealtimes are, you'll need to teach him. But do this gradually – it will take him some getting used to. Show your toddler that mealtimes are important family times that you love and value; let him see how much you enjoy sitting down to eat together, as a family or just with him. If you show your toddler your own good eating habits, it won't be long before he'll copy them. On the other hand, if you're stressed at mealtimes, your toddler will be too, so make sure you're as relaxed as possible. Switch off the TV and put your phone onto voicemail. Don't use his mealtime to load the dishwasher, write a 'to do' list or pack a lunch box. Spend the time together and when you talk to him, listen with your ears and eyes. Remember that little ones take time to eat, so allow him enough time to eat comfortably. Make meals a priority, and don't rush them. They're important events.

# Condensed idea
## Toddlers have unpredictable and messy eating habits as they struggle to eat independently

# 8 Who controls the TV remote?

**You may find yourself occasionally doing things you said you'd never do – such as letting your toddler sit in front of the TV for hours on end to avoid the inevitable tantrum when you switch it off. But you need to create 'screen rules' that will work now and for years to come.**

## Set the TV boundaries now

As your toddler grows up, she's likely to want to spend increasing amounts of time in front of a screen, watching TV or a DVD, or playing a computer game. If you negotiate the rules now, she will get into the habit of accepting clear boundaries, and it will make family life much easier in years to come.

What works for one parent when it comes to toddlers and TV may not work for another. This means that you're the only person who can decide what is right for you and your family. Once you focus on the issue of TV watching, you'll begin to make great decisions – the problem is that many of us don't stop to consider how we want the TV to be used. As a result, what usually happens is that the amount of TV a toddler watches gradually creeps up and up without the parents realizing it. When parents do stop to add up the amount of time their little one spends in front of a television screen, it's often much longer than they imagined. This is complicated by the fact that the more TV toddlers watch, the more they want to watch.

> He knows what buttons to press. #mumunderpressure

# Who's in charge of the TV?

Answer the following questions to find out who controls the TV zapper in your home. Is it you or your toddler? Count up the number of times you answer 'yes' or 'no'.

- Does your toddler watch whatever she likes?
- Is TV a reason things take longer – for example, when she's getting dressed?
- Does your toddler watch more TV than you want her to?
- Does your toddler watch programmes you've never seen?
- Do you ever give in to her TV demands because 'it's easier than arguing'?
- Do you let her watch TV at mealtimes?
- Does your toddler watch more TV than you do?

If you answered 'yes' to most questions, your toddler controls the TV remote. If you answered mostly 'no', you're in charge.

Parents sometimes unwittingly begin to use the TV more and more as a way to keep their toddler happy and occupied. It takes a strong will and commitment to avoid the easy route provided by this free babysitter. And you're not alone – this happens in most family homes, sometimes to the point where the television is on all the time from morning to night.

## Be creative

By setting a positive boundary in terms of screen time, your toddler will benefit in many ways. You'll be helping her to keep active and develop

healthy habits that will last a lifetime. You're showing her you value time with her away from the TV and she will learn to value that time too. Suggest games you can play together instead of watching TV. By creating time for her to do this – with you, other children and other adults – you're nurturing her natural creativity and the development of her communication and social skills. You're also creating opportunities for her to learn through play, which is the most powerful way for her to learn at this age. Creative games boost your child's confidence and self-belief, and she will love them. Children are often a lot better at letting their imagination run wild than the adults around them. TV and high-tech games have a strong appeal for children, but they can be isolating. Fun family games cost little and create memories that last forever.

## Make positive decisions

There are three things you need to decide about your toddler's TV habits: how long, when and where. First, decide how long each day you are happy for your toddler to be watching a screen. Just think about the total time per day at this stage. Then think about when you want her to watch it. Consider your days together and work out what kind of routine will work best for you. Plan what you want her to watch, and only give her choices that you are happy with. The best and easiest way to manage this is to record her favourite programmes so they're always available when you need them.

'Where?' might seem like an odd question, but now that many households have multiple screens of various kinds, it's one that's worth considering. You might decide to keep certain rooms in the house – such as her bedroom – as TV-free zones.

Make sure that you're always playing by your rules, not your toddler's, and be consistent. Many parents decide to keep the time before bed and before meals as TV-free time. There are no arguments about switching it off because it isn't on. Some decide to use screen time to motivate their toddler by letting her watch the TV when she has done something you want her to do. Every family is different, so do what works for you.

As you make your decisions, keep the whole issue in perspective. Life is a balance; it's not a case of putting the TV away in a cupboard, it's about taking control of how your toddler engages with it. As you'll know, there are benefits to great quality programming, as it can teach your toddler basic skills such as language and counting in a creative and engaging way. It can also help your toddler to see many things she might not see in her daily life, as it transports her to a world beyond your home.

## Your relationship with screens

Now is a good time to take a good look at your own TV, computer and mobile phone habits. If you treat the TV or your computer as an essential member of your family, it's likely your toddler will too. How important has that screen in the corner of the room, or that laptop, become in your life? You are your child's most powerful role model, so if you want her to cut down on screen time, make sure you cut down too. Set yourself some positive boundaries and your toddler will follow your lead.

## Condensed idea
### Make careful decisions about what your toddler can watch, then stick to them

# 9 'No!'

Sometimes, when asking your toddler to pick up a toy or clean her teeth, you may be met with total rebellion. It can seem as though your toddler's favourite word has suddenly become 'No!'. There are some practical strategies you can use to help her learn to cooperate.

## Being defiant is normal

All toddlers (and older children) are uncooperative at times. Defiance is common at this age as your little one tries to assert her independence. However, even though it's normal for your toddler to say 'No', it's also normal for you to feel stressed when she does. This may be because you're taking her refusal as a statement about your parenting style, but in fact, she simply wants to show you that she has a mind of her own and to test the limits of the boundaries on any issue – to see if you really are going to stick to them. So it's important (but tough) to be patient. Remember too, that while this is difficult for you, it's difficult for her too. It's a challenging phase, but it will pass.

> I said no and I mean no!
> #toddlerrulesok

## Why toddlers say 'No'

There are many reasons why your toddler may say no. She may be flexing her muscles and wanting to tell you that she has her own opinion about what she is going to do. Recognize the power of giving her choices; but only offer choices that are all good options, such as asking

'Do you want to put on your pyjamas or clean your teeth first?' at bed time. If you involve your toddler in the decision-making, she'll be much more likely to cooperate and you will have fewer battles.

A toddler may also say 'No' because she doesn't really understand what you are asking her to do; she's confused but she doesn't really have the language to explain this to you. This will make her even more frustrated and 'no' is a plain and simple word that she can yell at the top of her voice. It is also guaranteed to get mum or dad's attention. You can ease this problem by helping her to develop her language skills so that she can learn how to express her feelings. Once she can do this, you'll have a much better understanding of the issue and an opportunity to sort it out.

Sometimes toddlers say 'No' because a parent has asked them to do something and the job seems overwhelming. 'Tidy up your toys' may seem simple to you, but to her it may be a huge mountain to climb. She may not even want to begin, because she may be worried that it's too big for her to manage and there's a good chance she might fail. If you

# Helping your little rebel

It's good for toddlers to learn to say 'No' –
once they're teenagers you'll be glad that they
learned this necessary art. However, to avoid
every day becoming full of arguments, use one
of these top tips:

- Use statements. Say 'It's time for bed now'
  rather than 'Are you ready for bed?'. Don't
  ask questions that your toddler can reply to with a 'No'.
- Give clear and brief directions. She may say 'No' because she
  doesn't understand what you want.
- Give her a realistic time to do what you want her to do – if she
  can't manage in time, she may refuse to even start.
- Avoid idle threats; for example, 'If you don't come right away,
  I'm leaving you in the park.'
- Let your toddler have some control over what is happening.
  Let her get into her pushchair, for example, instead of being
  put in by you.
- Distract your toddler. Give her a toy or dance around the
  room with her. She'll often forget that she was about to start
  arguing with you.
- Describe how her behaviour makes you feel. Say 'I don't like
  to hear you moaning' instead of 'You are always moaning'.
- Give your toddler a five-minute warning so that she knows she
  will soon be putting her toys away, for instance. Toddlers need
  structure and they need to know what to expect.
- Be positive. Praise your toddler when she does cooperate;
  don't take it for granted.
- Learn to take 'No' in your stride.

think this is the case, suggest you do the task together. Break it down into chunks and make sure that each chunk is a 'can do' task for her. Remember, too, that your toddler may just be feeling tired or hungry. Even adults feel more negative and irritable in these states. Make sure your toddler has regular snacks, mealtimes and bedtimes to help avoid unnecessary refusals and resistance.

## Explain the consequences

If you have tried everything and your toddler continues to refuse to cooperate, keep calm. It's time for her to learn that actions have consequences. Remember that she is still little, so you need to be very clear about your rules for disobedience. Keep the rules simple and consistent so that she knows what to expect, and if you need to put them into action, make sure you do exactly what you said and explain the reason why you are doing it. It's important for her to know what makes her behaviour unacceptable – especially if it is for safety reasons. When all is said and done, move on.

## Say 'Yes' whenever you can

Your toddler learns from you, so make a real effort to keep your use of the word 'no' to an absolute minimum. It's easy to fall into bed at the end of the day feeling as though all you have done all day is moan and say 'No!' to your toddler. If you do that, your toddler will learn to do it too. Try to find lots of different ways of expressing how you are feeling, so your toddler learns how to express her feelings to you. You are her mentor. So each day, set yourself the goal of smiling more often than you frown, and saying 'Yes!' more often than you say 'No'.

## Condensed idea
### Try to work out what your toddler is really trying to say when she says 'No!'

# ⑩ Toddler unplugged

**At around the age of two, your toddler will discover her vocal muscles, and she'll be keen to show you just how loudly she can scream with them. This signals that it's time for you to cut your stress levels and turn down the volume, so that you can enjoy being a mum.**

## Noisy toddlers are experimenting

Family homes are naturally noisy, and when your toddler begins to pump up the volume, you'll really begin to feel that your home has no volume control. It may be exasperating, but all that's happened is that your toddler has found something she can do and enjoy – creating sound that can be very high and very loud. What fun! While you may wince at every screech, toddlers are usually totally unaware of just how loud they are being. This can be particularly stressful for parents when toddlers decide to scream at the top of their voices in public. Toddlers also have very limited communication skills, but screaming at the top of her voice is one way she knows she'll definitely get your immediate and full attention.

> Going deaf. How do I turn down the volume on this boy? #earplugsplease

## Speak more quietly

You can't unplug your toddler, but you can make sure you have volume control. However, before you even start to deal with your toddler, it's time to sort out your own volume levels. Be honest with yourself. Most parents are surprised to find out just how noisy they are, and think it's just their children who raise the decibel level. Your toddler will take her lead from you, so if your normal noise levels are unacceptable, hers will be too. If yours are acceptable, then hers are more likely to be too.

You may not even have noticed that you have developed some undesirable noisy habits. For example, how often do you have the TV or radio on when you're not really listening to it? How often do you communicate with your toddler when you're in a different room from her? Is your mobile phone always on? How often do you increase your

## Quiet fun

You need to help your toddler communicate at normal levels, instead of shouting loudly (she'll find this especially tempting when she really wants to be heard). Try these practical ideas on your toddler and you'll soon notice a difference:

- Play whispering games together. Talk quietly so that she has to really listen. Ask her to have a go at whispering too. Toddlers find this difficult, but they'll always rise to a challenge.
- Reinforce the times you want her to reduce her volume by turning the dial on her belly button as if it is a volume control. She'll love it.
- When your toddler starts to get noisy, encourage her to do an activity that is noisy – put on some music, sing a song with you or play a musical instrument. It will still be noisy, but more fun, and you will be channelling all that noise in a very positive and practical way.

volume to be heard over your toddler? How often do you shout to tell your toddler to stop being so noisy? Most parents would admit to most, if not all, of these. By focusing on some of these points, you will be raising your awareness of just how noisy you can be. These are all areas you can change because you're in control of them, and by lowering the general noise levels in the house, you are more likely to lower the noise levels of your toddler too.

## Say what you want her to do

Make sure you use the positive approach to directives, rather than the negative one: tell your toddler what you do want her to do, rather than what you don't want her to do. This will always be much more effective. It will also help you to focus on achieving what you want. Also, make sure that you're not asking her to do something that you are doing differently yourself.

| Do say... | Don't say (or shout)... |
|---|---|
| • 'Talk quietly.' | • 'Don't shout.' |
| • 'Look at me when I'm talking so I can see your beautiful eyes.' | • 'I know you're not listening – you're watching TV.' |
| • 'I can hear what you're saying if you take it in turns.' | • 'I can't hear a thing if you're all shouting at once.' |
| • 'I will listen to you if you talk to me.' | • 'I'm not going to do anything if you shout.' |
| • 'Look see if you can do this' (wiggle your fingers) | • 'Stop banging on the table!' |

# Indoor and outdoor voices

Your toddler needs a good teacher. She won't know what level of volume is appropriate until you make it really clear to her. She will need to learn the difficult concept of using a different volume depending on context, so be patient with her as she learns. Introduce your toddler to the idea of her 'inside' and 'outside' voice. Show her what you mean: have fun showing her how you talk quietly inside the home but can talk loudly or even shout outside. Sing loudly in the park. Or shout to one another from the swings. This is a simple idea that really works. If you reinforce what you want, she will begin to learn what you expect.

Help her to practise volume control by making sure she is in the same room as you when she wants to say something. Don't let her get into the habit of using her 'outside voice' inside, just because she is in a different room. And make sure you don't fall into that trap too. If you're in someone else's house, or a shop or café and she begins to get noisy and won't be quiet, take her outside where it's appropriate for her to use that louder volume. Then ask her to change her voice so she can come back indoors, talking quietly. Make sure you praise your toddler or give her a sticker each time she uses her 'inside' and 'outside' voices correctly.

## Condensed idea
**Toddlers don't realize how loud they are –
they're usually just having fun**

# (11) Stress-free evenings

It's important for your sanity – and your toddler's wellbeing – that he goes to bed at a reasonable time and has a good night's rest. But often the real challenge is getting your toddler into bed. This chapter will give you some simple strategies to avoid bedtime battles.

## Three reasons for non-cooperation

If you haven't already done so, this is an important time to establish a bedtime routine for your toddler. A great sleep will mean he'll be more energized and have more fun when he's playing and learning. Unfortunately, he's likely to resist your best efforts because he's incapable of thinking in the longterm. However, once you understand what's going through your toddler's mind, it will help you to handle his behaviour well.

> I've read six stories already but Jamie looks wide awake. I'm the one yawning! #hoarsedad

There are three main reasons that toddlers don't want to go to bed. The first is that life's just too much fun and he doesn't want to miss out. Your toddler will be totally convinced that while he's having to settle down in bed, you and the rest of the world are all partying. A calm bedtime routine that he looks forward to will help this idea to subside.

Second, your toddler doesn't want to give in to you. Bedtime is a great opportunity to assert his independence. If your toddler feels involved in the decision-making, he's much more likely to settle down well. Let him make some simple choices (with two options) as he prepares for bed – which pair of pyjamas to wear, what colour toothbrush to use or which book to read. Having a say will help him feel important.

Third – and this is an especially sweet thing to remember – when your toddler goes to bed, he misses you. If he's upset about you leaving once you've said goodnight, he may be trying his luck or he may just

# Top tips for a great bedtime routine

Here are some simple tactics for you to use to make your toddler's bedtime routine enjoyable for both of you:

- Make sure your toddler has an active day and uses up lots of energy so that he'll be ready to sleep.
- Avoid sugary snacks or drinks near bedtime.
- Avoid letting your toddler watch TV before bedtime.
- Keep your routine simple. Make it achievable for you and for him.
- Be consistent. Aim to start the bedtime routine at the same time every day.
- Give clear instructions and avoid questions and negotiation. Don't say: 'Do you want to clean your teeth?' Do say: 'It's time to clean our teeth. We always do it before we go to bed.'
- Play by your rules – not his. Don't give in. If he says he's not tired, tell him that is okay, but it's still time for bed.
- Make good use of his bedroom at different times of the day so that he regards it as a place where he feels happy and safe.

want to be with you. 'Goodnight' can sometimes seem as though it's 'goodbye'. Night-time can also be a bit scary for little children, making them reluctant to be away from their protective parents. Take your time reading to him and tucking him in so that he feels special, and reassure him that you are close by.

## Toddlers love routines

You're the best person to decide what to put into your toddler's routine. The main thing is to keep it simple. Your toddler will soon get to know what to expect and this will help him feel secure and relaxed. He will be much more challenging if he's tired and grumpy, so start early and allow plenty of time for his bedtime ritual.

Bath, books and bed are the three basic ingredients of a good routine. Toddlers usually love a dip in a warm bath and it will begin to calm him down. Add some bubbles or toys and enjoy this relaxing time with him. Then let him have a say in what pyjamas to wear. If your toddler takes ages getting into them, challenge him to put them on before you count to 10 – or invest in a giant egg-timer. They're a great visual way to teach him about time. Get him into the habit of brushing his teeth as early as you can. You'll have to do a lot of the work until he can do it properly – but let him have a go first. Clean your teeth at the same time if that helps him to see how to do it well.

All children love sharing books with mum or dad and it can become a special time for both of you. Let him pick a couple of stories, but beware! Toddlers love repetition so be prepared to read the same book every night for a week. Have a cuddle together and enjoy the one-on-one time. Avoid stories with aliens or monsters and don't go mad with any acting out – that's great for daytime reading, but you should use this time to calm your toddler – not rev him up.

Have a clear end to your routine so your toddler knows you are going to leave and that he is expected to go to sleep on his own. Finish reading, tuck him into bed, turn on the night-light and a soothing CD if you want to use music to help him feel relaxed and comforted. Take a few minutes to talk to him, perhaps saying what you've loved about spending time with him during that day. Then say goodnight and leave the room. If he gets upset, tell him you'll come back in a few minutes – and keep your promise – but keep your visits short and boring.

## Create a visual map

You could take some pictures of your toddler at each stage of his bedtime routine and put them up on his wall – creating a visual map will enable him to see what you want to achieve together in his bedtime ritual. You can laminate it so that he can tick it with a marker – or turn it into a simple sticker chart. This turns bedtime into a simple game with an obvious end (and probably a big kiss!).

# Condensed idea
## Bedtime routines can help calm excited toddlers and make evenings less stressful

# 12  Solving sleep problems

You've got a great evening routine in place and all seems to be going smoothly. But just when you breathe a sigh of relief because your toddler's sleeping through the night – she begins to wake up. The good news is that night-waking is a habit that can be broken.

## Follow your instinct

Your toddler's sleeping habits will change during the first three years, but one of the most difficult things for parents to deal with is the sudden return of broken nights. However, if you know it is going to happen and expect it, you'll cope better when it does. The next step is to start finding ways to shift her back to an easier sleep pattern.

There are lots of reasons why your toddler may begin to wake in the night. Have there been any changes in her daily routine? Is she feeling overwhelmed by starting nursery, getting used to a new brother or sister or getting used to potty training? Is she having nightmares because she's afraid of the dark or thinks there's a monster in the wardrobe? Is she feeling ill or cutting a tooth? Listen to your gut instinct and go with it – you'll be absolutely right. Once you have identified possible explanations, you'll feel better equipped to cope.

## Look for an explanation

Check to see if there's a physical reason why your toddler may be waking up. If she's complaining of mouth pain or earache, or there's something else that's affecting her and you want to get some professional advice, make an appointment to talk to your doctor. If your toddler is in good

shape physically but still waking up during the night, explore other reasons for her broken nights, such as anxiety. Is your toddler worried about something? Often minor changes in daily routine can have a big impact on a small child. Or she may be picking up on the mood of mum or dad. If you're worried about anything, it is very likely that your child can sense your preoccupation – or perhaps she's heard a row between you and your partner. All these things can affect a child's sleeping too. Step into your toddler's pyjamas and see the world through her eyes. Is there anything that may be going on in her life that is making her feel a little overwhelmed?

If there is, the best thing for you to do is give her lots of cuddles and reassurance. Acknowledge her feelings, because they are important to her – don't dismiss them, saying there's nothing to worry about. Giving her your time and love will help her to feel more secure, and if she's feeling secure, she's more likely to feel restful at night-time too.

## Toddler nightmares

Your toddler has a vivid imagination – she may begin to experience nightmares and find it hard to distinguish between what's real and imaginary. You can't prevent bad dreams, but you can reduce the chances of them happening by making sure you don't read scary books

## Seven-day solution to night-waking

Sleep training is tough, but if you stick to this plan for seven nights, you'll see a difference. It only works if you are consistent, so begin when you are feeling strong enough to stand your ground.

- Give your toddler action-packed days and don't let her nap, especially in the afternoon, unless she really needs one.
- Don't rush the bedtime routine. Start it slightly earlier than before and take your time, so it's slow and relaxed.
- Leave the room before she goes to sleep. She'll learn that you expect her to go to sleep by herself and will then have confidence to do this on her own if she wakes up.
- Let her choose a special soft toy to take to bed for company. It'll comfort her if she wakes.
- If she cries out, don't go immediately unless you are worried she is sick. Wait a few minutes to see if she settles herself down again.
- If you need to go in to reassure her, keep the lights low and talk quietly. Leave her in bed, don't pick her up.
- When she's calm, leave the room. If she cries again, wait a little before you return. If you feel comfortable, leave longer gaps between visits, and keep them brief and boring.

or let her watch DVDs with monsters in them too close to bedtime. If she does have a nightmare, reassure her that it is a dream and that it is not real. If she wants to talk about what happened in the dream, let her, but don't force her. The important thing is to let her know that you are taking her feelings seriously, and that she is safe.

## What to do with early risers

Some toddlers wake very early. It may help if she has thick curtains or blinds in her bedroom that don't let in the light, which may be what is waking her up. If you do have an early riser on your hands, you could encourage her to stay in her bedroom until a particular time, by teaching her to recognise when the hands on the clock are pointing at the 'right' numbers. This is a good introduction to helping her learn to tell the time. You could also let your child choose some safe 'early morning' toys that she can play with when she wakes.

> Bags under eyes becoming huge suitcases. Must find solution! #needsomesleep

## Ask for help

If you have tried everything and your child is still having sleep problems, make an appointment to talk to your doctor or your health visitor. They'll be able to give you lots of practical advice. You and your toddler need a good night's sleep – so do something about it today.

## Condensed idea
### Sleep patterns change, but check for an explanation if your toddler suddenly begins waking a lot at night

# (13) Sibling rivalry

**Having a son or daughter is one thing. But when you go from one child to two, it's a whole new experience for all of the family. Learning to handle tantrums, resolve conflicts and create sibling harmony is tough but important for both you and your children.**

## Explosions are normal

With two children, there's definitely too much to do and never quite enough mum to go round. Not only that, your toddler may have started to throw the mother of all tantrums. It's natural for him to shout and stamp his feet when he has to share your love with a brother or sister. How would you feel if your partner turned up one day with another adult to share the family home? You'd struggle. That's exactly how your toddler feels. He's had his parents all to himself – and now he's expected to share your attention. It's a difficult thing for him to come to terms with, so one moment they may be playing happily together and the next, war breaks out. This is, however, a normal part of family life.

## Sibling rivalry can be good

Sibling rivalry is stressful for everyone involved, but it does have its benefits. For brothers and sisters, learning to compromise and negotiate is an important part of growing up. There's nothing like having to share the TV remote or a favourite toy to put their social and communication skills to the test. These are life skills they'll use for many years to come. With good parenting, they'll learn to pull together and to support each other – and to support you. It will be this powerful family bond that will help all of you through any family challenges that lie ahead.

# Don't compare siblings

Each of your children is unique and each has his or her own special qualities. It's great to spend time together as a family, but also to spend time with each child on their own. Use the time to really tune in to what makes them tick as individuals. It can be very tempting, but don't compare one child with another in a positive or negative way. Saying to one child 'Why can't you be as good as your sister?' is quite likely to have the opposite effect to the one you are hoping for. Avoid saying things like 'You should know better because you are older.' Yes he is, but he is still very little. It is not, for example, realistic to expect him to share his toys with his sister all of the time just because she is younger.

> I need a clone! Seems like there's never enough mum to go round. #muminthemiddle

# Top tips for sibling harmony

These practical ideas will encourage teamwork and help cut down on sibling fights or bad feelings:

- Acknowledge your toddler's feelings. When he says 'I hate my sister', don't rebuke him with 'You don't mean that' – because in the heat of that moment he probably does. Don't make him feel guilty for emotions that are perfectly normal; instead, help him to deal with them.
- Go with your gut instinct about whether and when to intervene. When they argue, don't step in right away. Wait a few minutes to see if they resolve it themselves.
- Explain how you want them to play together – instead of how you don't. Instead of saying 'Don't argue' say: 'Why don't you take it in turns to throw the ball?'
- Give them attention for working well as a team, not attention for arguing.
- Be specific when you praise your toddler for behaviour you want to encourage. Say: 'You're being a great brother helping your sister by holding her hand as we walk' instead of just 'Good boy.'
- Encourage them to do things together like team games, cooking with you, laying the table or putting their toys away. Set them challenges to complete as a team.
- Have fun together. It's the very best way to create sibling harmony.
- Try putting them together in the same bedroom. Having each other for company at night-time can help form a close bond.

# Be fair and avoid favouritism

Establish family rules that everyone agrees are fair and be consistent in applying them – start as you mean to go on. When children are arguing, focus on the solution to the argument, not on every detail that's being presented (you're likely to hear lots of 'She did this!' and 'He did that!'). Blame isn't helpful and, at the end of the day, you want them to learn how to sort out issues for themselves and play together happily. If they both want to watch different things on TV, teach them how to take it in turns. Whenever they want different things, encourage them to compromise, and help them to think of ways to do this.

The one time that you will need to step in decisively is when an argument between siblings gets physical. Your children must learn that hitting, biting and kicking is unacceptable. Remember too, that toddlers can hurt babies accidentally – sometimes through nothing more than an over-enthusiastic hug – so never leave a toddler alone with an infant.

# Set a good example

The very best way to teach your children to negotiate, compromise and see things from another's perspective is to do these things yourself. So if you want to watch sport and your partner wants to watch a soap, consider this a perfect time to demonstrate the art of compromise, and allow your children to see this negotiation in action. This is especially important because if you ask your children to do anything you're not prepared to do yourself, it won't happen. But if you do it, they'll follow suit. Your children learn what to do from watching you.

# Condensed idea
## Sibling rivalry is normal, but be careful of doing or saying things that may make it worse

# 14 'I don't want clothes!'

A toddler is usually ready to start learning how to dress herself at around two years old. It's an exciting milestone for her, but there will be times when she will stubbornly refuse to put on her clothes. Avoid wardrobe wars by using a few simple tips.

## Avoid the rush

Getting dressed is one of the perfect times for your little one to assert her independence. Unfortunately many of us are usually in a hurry in the mornings and if your toddler knows you want her to get dressed as quickly as possible, that's usually the time she'll take as long as she can. She wants you to know that she has a say in what's going on in her life – and this is a great way to demonstrate it. Plus toddlers just don't like change and will buck against it at every opportunity, and it's not hard to understand why. Your daughter's quite comfortable in her pyjamas, so why would she want to get out of them?

Give yourself time rather than rushing towards a deadline. Wake her up a little earlier so that you both have as much time as possible in order for you both to enjoy her dressing routine – not dread it. Her concept of time is different from yours; you may think that 10 minutes will give her lots of time to get dressed but, for a toddler learning this skill for the first time, it doesn't. You've had years of practice so remember that she'll take much longer than you think, even when she's trying her hardest. Whilst her fingers are enthusiastic, they can act a bit like sausages on the end of her hands. So be patient and be realistic about what you expect her to achieve, and give her lots of praise when she succeeds at even the smallest of milestones.

# Fun not frantic

You may just want to get the whole 'getting dressed thing' over and done with, but your toddler will enjoy spending dressing time having fun with you. It is worth noting that the more enjoyable you make it for her, the easier it will be for you, as she will be more responsive. You can avoid struggles in the morning by helping her lay out her outfit the night

## Getting dressed without stress

If dressing is becoming problematic, try one (or more) of the following ideas:

- Make it easy to get results. Choose clothes with Velcro® fastenings, elastic waists and slip-on shoes. Avoid clothes that are tricky or tight. Once she's cracked these, she'll soon have the confidence to move on to more challenging zips and buttons.
- Don't ask questions that she may say 'No' to. Give her a clear and confident direction and explain your reasoning. Instead of saying, 'Do you want to wear tights today?' say: 'You are wearing warm tights today because it is very cold outside.'
- Distract her if she starts to become obstinate. Give her a toy to play with while you help her on with her clothes.
- Show her what to do; for example, demonstrate how to put a jumper on by putting your arms through first and then pulling it over your head.
- Let her practise dressing and undressing her favourite teddy.
- Put her favourite music on so that you can sing along as you dress.

before. Let her be involved in choosing what she's going to wear. Keep this simple and limit her choices to two. Make life easy by giving her a choice of jumper or T-shirt, for example, while you choose the rest.

You could make this activity even more fun for your toddler by asking her to lie down on a large piece of paper or card and drawing around her so that she has a life-size outline of herself. Each evening, she can lay her clothes out on the cut-out so it's all ready for the morning (afterwards you can roll it up for easy storage). Another way to help her would be to lay the clothes out on her bed – from left to right – in the order

> Stella is torn – socks or tights? Red or blue? Or green? #waitingmum

she needs to put them on. It's not essential but it will certainly help, and having a system like this will develop her organizational skills. You may see her begin to adopt a similar approach in other areas.

When your toddler takes off her pyjamas in the morning, encourage her to put them where you want them to go – on a chair, for instance – rather than dropping them on the floor for you to pick up. It may take a little longer to teach her this now, but you'll be glad you stuck to your guns when you realize that even as a teenager, she's automatically putting her clothes away.

## Praise and rewards

Visual charts with stickers and stars work well for encouraging good dressing habits. Give your toddler a star for each piece of clothing she puts on and introduce an 'end of the week star ceremony' where she can swap her stars for a reward (such as going swimming). When it comes to rewards, think about time, not money. If you are happy for your toddler to watch TV in the morning, you could tell her that she can watch TV for 20 minutes when she has finished getting dressed. The important thing is to institute and stick to a rule that works for you.

# Lose the battle, win the war

There will be occasions when your toddler refuses to get dressed. Try to keep calm and dress her without saying anything. If she's getting your attention, she'll carry on being obstinate. If she absolutely refuses to get out of her pyjamas, take her to nursery in them (with some clothes in case she changes her mind when she gets there – which she probably will). It's good for your toddler to learn that actions have consequences. Make sure you let her choose what to wear sometimes. You may want her to go out beautifully co-ordinated, but does it really matter if she's wearing a creative combination of colours and mismatching socks? As long as she's not too hot or too cold, she'll be fine.

## Condensed idea
### Give your toddler lots of time and practice when learning to get dressed

# (15) Easy toilet training

**Every toddler will eventually get the hang of using the toilet, but be prepared – toilet training is a messy business. Give it a go when you have got the time, patience and energy. The more positive and relaxed you are, the more successful you will be.**

## Is your toddler ready?

There's no right age to start toilet training. Every toddler is different and some will get the hang of it much earlier than others. Boys often take longer than girls, but in general, most children are aged between two and three when they start. Don't feel under pressure to start training because other parents are doing it. Your gut instinct will tell you when your child is ready. Look out for the signs; these include showing interest in the toilet, telling you he wants to wee or poo or pulling off his nappies.

Make the toilet a more friendly place by providing a much-loved companion (such as a teddy), sitting on his own potty.

Choose a good time to begin toilet training, when he's healthy and not struggling with teething or feeling under the weather. You both need to be on top form to make this work! Also, make sure it doesn't coincide with a change in your toddler's daily routine, such as a change of schedule or childcare, as this will also have an impact on how successful you are. Training during summer months is helpful because you can let your little one run around with a bare bottom.

## Making preparations

Before starting, decide whether you want to use a potty or would rather attach a training seat to your toilet. Some parents use a potty first and move on to the toilet, while others go straight to the toilet – with the help of a child seat and a step. Either way is fine, so choose what feels right for you. A week or so before starting, talk to your toddler about what you are going to do. Sharing a fun book or DVD about using the potty provides a good opportunity for

> One day he will go to the toilet alone! One day soon, hopefully. #muminwaiting

chatting about what's going to happen. Guide him through example too – good habits are caught, not taught – so take him with you when you go to the toilet and show him how it's done. When you think it's time for him to start using the potty or toilet, take him shopping to choose some pants he really likes – it's amazing what an incentive can do! On the day you intend to start, let him choose a new pair of pants to wear. The more involved he feels in the process, the more successful you're likely to be.

## Regular visits

Consistency is key here, as it is for much of toddler training. Sit your toddler on his potty or toilet at regular intervals. Remember that young children don't like sitting still for long, so help him to stay there by chatting to him or reading a story. It's best to teach both boys and girls to wee sitting down (boys can learn to manage it standing up later). It might seem logical to keep asking your toddler if he needs a wee, but this can become distressing. Instead, give him clear direction, by saying, for example, 'Have a wee and then I am going to take you out to play in the garden.' Whatever you do, don't push him. If you put him under

# Three problems, three solutions

There are three main reasons that toddlers take longer to master toilet training: fear, lack of familiarity and inconsistency of approach. Before you begin, bear the following points in mind:

- The toilet can frighten toddlers. It's big and hard, and it makes a loud noise. Try giving your toddler a 'toilet teddy' who sits with him. When you begin the training, don't flush until your toddler has left the bathroom (give him time to get used to the sound).
- Some toddlers are trained at home but not able to use the toilet when out and about. This is perfectly natural. Have part of the routine that is portable, such as singing the same song as at home; this will help him feel comfortable.
- If your toddler has got the hang of it but now keeps having accidents, take time to understand what's causing this and give him lots of reassurance. It may be that you're confusing him by occasionally using nappies. Or perhaps you began training by making it exciting, but now the excitement has died down. If you think this might be the case, find a new way to motivate him, such as a sticker chart. When he has five stickers, give him a treat. Most importantly, helping your toddler to feel secure by giving him lots of cuddles will help his return to the toilet.

pressure when he's not ready, he'll get upset and tantrums will follow. Learning to use the potty or toilet probably feels like a 'must' in your head, but if this is the message you send at the beginning of training, you're likely to meet with resistance. Keep it low-key and without pressure. Make the experience positive for him, by adopting a favourite song for your toddler to listen to when he's on the toilet, or giving him a good book to look at. When he uses the toilet successfully, praise him. Having a toilet sticker chart in the bathroom can work wonders. But don't go overboard or he may feel under pressure to perform, and deflated when accidents happen.

## Accidents will happen!

Toilet training will take time. Some toddlers take weeks, others months, and bladder control usually comes after bowel control. It's also perfectly normal for a toddler to be dry during the day, but not at night; it can take a lot longer to be dry through the night. While your child is learning potty training, 'accidents' are inevitable. It's natural to feel frustrated when this happens, but try to stay calm and clean it up without being negative. This is all new to him. If he does have an accident, sit him on the toilet afterwards to show him where he should have gone. Sometimes when he says he wants a wee, he means 'Right now!' and he won't be able to hold on long enough to make it to the toilet. That 'holding on' takes training. When this happens, leave him in his wet pants for a few minutes (no longer) and he'll make a bigger effort to make it to the toilet next time. If your toddler has lots of accidents, it may mean that he's not quite ready to shift to toilet use just yet, so go back to nappies for a while and try again later. It does not mean you or he have failed. It just means the time is not quite right.

## Condensed idea
### Be prepared, consistent, calm and reassuring about toilet training

# 16 'I won't share!'

Your toddler will find it really hard to share, whether it's sharing mum or dad, or her favourite toy. She's not being selfish, she is just acting her age. She thinks she is the centre of the universe and everything belongs to her. Sharing is a skill that takes time to learn.

## Give sharing a high-five

It's usual for every toddler to throw a tantrum over sharing, and it will take lots of your time and patience, but it's worth persisting. Learning to share will not only help your toddler develop important social skills that will last a lifetime, but will also teach your child how to compromise, take turns and negotiate. These are all great life skills. In addition, it also teaches children how to cope with disappointment, which is a skill many grown-ups admit to still perfecting!

Sharing is a tough concept and your behaviour will play an important part in her understanding. Take every opportunity you can to show her what it means to share. You can start by offering your toddler a bite of your banana or sandwich. As you are taking it in turns to eat, use the word 'share' so that she understands the relationship between the word and the action. Say: 'Would you like to share my banana?' as you offer it to her. If you praise her for sharing well, she'll soon realize that it makes you happy and gives her positive attention, and she'll begin to do it naturally by herself. As well as praising her with words, create a special thing to do when she shares, such as sharing high-five. This can work wonders. It can also become a sign that you signal to her when she's playing with others and you want her to share, but without overtly telling her to do so.

# Refusing to share

Every parent knows just how embarrassing it can be when a toddler is on a playdate with a friend – and their child stamps her foot, grabs the toy she wants to play with and shouts, 'No! It's mine!' If there is something she really wants, she'll find it very hard to wait her turn and will try to get it any way she can. It's not a reflection on you or on her. She's just learning that she can't have everything and she doesn't like it.

## Top tips to encourage sharing

Helping your toddler to learn to share will be one of your toughest parenting assignments. Here are some practical ideas to help you:

- Play games that involve taking turns and sharing. Build a block tower and take it in turns to add one block at a time.
- Encourage your toddler to 'share' with her teddies and toys.
- Set your kitchen timer for five minutes to help playing toddlers learn to share a toy by swapping toys every time it rings.
- Point out good examples of sharing when you are reading books or watching a DVD or TV.
- Ask your toddler to look out for good examples of sharing and tell you about them. When you see her sharing, give her specific praise: 'It was very kind of you to let Sally have a go on your scooter – good sharing!'
- Enlist an older sibling's help. They'll love the responsibility.
- When you are feeling frustrated, count to three and remember that you don't go around sharing your iPod with other adults in the nursery playground.

If another toddler is coming to play, give your toddler the opportunity to put away three of her special toys, telling her she can choose the ones she really doesn't want to share. Make it clear to her that, while she doesn't have to share her three special toys, the ones left out are for everyone to play with. She may have difficulty deciding which three are the crucial ones, so be prepared for this decision to take some time!

One important first step that your toddler will go through is showing her toys to friends. She may still hang on to one of her toys and not actually let it go, but her demonstration of her toys is still a positive step towards learning to share. So watch out for this behaviour and be sure to praise it with words and your special signal (such as a high-five).

If it looks as though your toddler is refusing to share her toys, keep calm and don't rush in, however tempting that might be. It's important to give her a little time to try to work things out herself. If she's not sharing, the other children will soon show your toddler that they're not happy and she'll have other grumpy toddlers on her hands. While it may take time, and many similar occasions, she will eventually understand that her friends are happy when she shares with them, and if they're happy, she will be too.

When you decide you are going to intervene, acknowledge your toddler's feelings and tell her that you are disappointed with her behaviour (not her!). Tell her how you want to feel ('It will make me feel happy to see you being kind and sharing'), but don't engage in a power struggle. Show her

> Uh oh. India insists on 'sharing' my mobile. #modeldad

clearly that her actions have a consequence by removing the toy for five minutes, while explaining why you are doing this. You can then let her have the toy back again, giving her another chance to share it.

Whatever you do, don't give your toddler lots of attention because she is not sharing. Only give her attention for behaviour you want to see repeated, not behaviour that's undesirable. If you can see that on this occasion she really isn't going to share, don't put yourself under pressure. Change direction and try a different tactic. Get your toddler and her friend to do something completely different, like drawing or dancing – something they can both do without having to share favourite possessions. If your toddler continues to struggle with sharing, don't avoid playdates. The more practice she gets, the easier she will find it.

## Don't expect her to share everything

Be realistic. If your toddler has siblings, don't expect her to share all her toys with them just because they are her brother or sister. It is better to let her make some of her own decisions and assert her independence. Ask her to choose a selection of toys that they can share with her and keep some that are special for her. She's important too.

## Condensed idea
### Sharing doesn't come naturally – it's a useful social skill that must be learned

# 17 Supermarket sanity

You're at the checkout when your toddler grabs a bag of sweets. You go to put them back, but she grips with superhuman strength and throws a tantrum that can be heard miles away. Shopping with a toddler can be very stressful, so it's good to have some strategies ready.

## Wanting his own way

The supermarket is a great place for your toddler to assert his independence, especially when there are so many goodies on display. He is probably thinking that this is a battle worth winning! He also knows you're in a rush and won't make a fuss when everyone is looking. He only has to demonstrate his iron will and you'll give in – then he'll get what he wants. This situation has a lot to do with the fact that a toddler lives in the moment; he sees something he wants and he wants it right now. He's not interested in the cost or in 'E' numbers, and he may have limited means of communication, but he can get his message across loud and clear. So don't take it personally when he brings a display crashing down with his flailing feet. He's trying to tell you something – and he's just got your total attention. The best thing to do is to go for damage limitation: keep him in the trolley, rather than wandering the aisles. While it's part of the role of a parent to multi-task, this is one situation where you need to keep your mind on the job in hand (shopping). It's important that you stay in the driving seat.

> Toddler happy in trolley, but I lost it over chocolate shortage. Need to grow up. #changingplaces

# Be prepared

Don't be surprised if your toddler throws the baked beans out of the supermarket trolley when you're under pressure to fit in a quick shop before feeding him. If he is tired or hungry, he'll get scratchy and create a fuss, so try to go at a time when he's feeling energized and full. The same can be said for you too! If you're tired and hungry, you'll also find the whole shopping experience more stressful. Although it's not always possible in a busy family life to go shopping at the perfect moment, do what you can to plan a time that's good for both you and your little one so that at least you're both relaxed at the start.

Another reason that your toddler may play up in the supermarket is that he's bored; the average attention span of a three-year-old is just three minutes. So go prepared with toys and healthy snacks to distract him, and always carry a clean nappy, wet wipes and a change of clothes in case of any accidents. To make your trip as quick and efficient as possible, make a list before you go. Not only will you not have to drag your toddler down every aisle of the supermarket to make sure you have everything, it will also mean that when you get distracted by your toddler you won't forget your essentials and go home without any bread or milk.

# Avoiding trolley tantrums

While it's just shopping to you, it's a totally different ball game for your toddler, so try to see life from his side of the trolley. This will help you to handle (or avoid) challenging situations better. After all, what toddler wouldn't want to grab at all those bags of sweets just within reach?

## Supermarket strategies

Take the stress out of shopping this week with one of these ideas:

- Think positive. If you're tense, ho will he, If you're calm, he'll be more likely to relax too.
- Make the trip fun. Keep him occupied and develop his language skills by talking to him as you go down the aisle. He loves the sound of your voice (and his own, of course!).
- Play supermarket-I-spy using colours or shapes. Ask things like 'Can you see something red?' or 'Can you see pasta that looks like a butterfly?'
- Let him hold the packets that are safe and fun for him to get his hands on.
- Give him a job. Ask him to be your 'little helper' and spot the things you want to buy.
- Give him a special supermarket trolley toy or book – one he can play with only on a shopping trip. Keep them in a special box in the boot of the car.
- Ask him to choose a fresh fruit or vegetable he likes the look of and let him help you prepare it for dinner.
- When you've finished, tell your toddler one thing you've enjoyed about spending time shopping with him.

Look out for the warning signs of growing irritation and distract him as soon as any crop up. For example, whizz over to the flower section and say: 'Come and smell these beautiful flowers' to avoid a tantrum. It's important to play by your rules – not your toddler's. If you give in to his demands because he screams for the packet of cereal with a particular cartoon character on it, that's what he'll do every time. And remember that although supermarket trolley rage can bring out the worst in your toddler, it can probably bring out the worst in you, too. A tantrum – yours or his – is always much more stressful when it happens in public.

If your toddler does have a tantrum, don't waste time feeling like a failure. You're not. Those other shoppers staring your way aren't thinking 'bad mum', they're sympathizing because they know exactly what you're going through. Keep calm and say to yourself: 'I can handle this'. You have a choice: you can either let him scream while you carry on shopping (the lack of attention might make him stop), or you can lift him out of the trolley, calmly and firmly, and take him outside for a few minutes. A change of scene and some fresh air may be all he needs to calm down.

## Three ways to do it differently

If you and your toddler find supermarket shopping stressful, change the way you do it. Avoid supermarket rush-hours; try shopping on a different day or at a different time when the supermarket is less busy. Or ask your partner or a friend to look after your toddler while you shop (you can always return the favour). Or do it all online! This can really take the pressure off, not least because all the heavy stuff will be delivered straight to your door. Doing your shopping online also creates more time for having fun with your toddler, doing things you'd both rather be doing.

## Condensed idea
### Take the time to put your toddler in the mood for shopping

# 18 Nursery door tantrums

**Your toddler's started going to nursery but drop-offs are stressful as she screams when you leave her. Her key worker assures you she's always fine within minutes, but you still feel guilty all day. This is a common problem and there are some practical steps you can take to help.**

## Stressful goodbyes

When children cry and parents feel unable to help, it can be incredibly stressful. Dropping your child off at nursery is a good example of this. The stress is increased by the fact that a time limit is imposed on your goodbyes to each other, so you may often be forced to leave while your child is still crying – a heartbreaking scenario that most parents will have had to endure at one time or another. However, there are

> Howling again at playgroup. Me, not her! #guiltymum

reasons why your toddler may scream, cling on to you for dear life, beg you to stay or complain she's feeling sick as you approach the nursery door. And understanding those reasons will help you develop a practical action plan to cope with it.

Going to nursery is a major milestone in your toddler's life – and yours too. It's the beginning of an adventure for her and the start of 'time off as a mum or dad' for you, but it can also cause anxieties for both of you. If you can find a way to manage your anxiety and stress, your toddler is more likely to manage hers better too. Children are quick to pick up on how you're feeling and will often mirror your behaviour.

# Fear of anxiety or separation

Your child may be worried about starting nursery. Toddlers love routine and security, and they don't enjoy change. There are lots of things that you can do to help her. For example, walk past the nursery before she begins and let her see the children playing in the playground. Or talk to her about the exciting activities she can do there. Focus on the ones she loves and tell her what fun she's going to have. Read books with positive stories about children starting nursery and making new friends.

The fear of being separated from mum or dad is common for children starting nursery. Your toddler wants to be independent but the thought of spending time away from you in a new environment may unnerve her. She doesn't want to leave the love and security you give her. One very helpful thing that you can do to prepare her for the separation is to arrange for her to start spending short, regular times away from you, perhaps with a friend or family member. Just half an hour once or twice a week will make a difference.

## Classmate worries

She could be trying to tell you that she's nervous about mixing with her classmates. Being in a room full of new children can be overwhelming. We've all been to parties where we've ended up talking to strangers when we'd rather be at home watching TV. Your toddler may feel the same. In the run-up to starting, create opportunities for her to spend time with other toddlers, such as taking her to a toddler group or a story-telling session at your local library.

Lots of toddlers cry because of something they've experienced at nursery. She may have got into an argument with a friend, been teased by another child or been part of something that felt frightening. If you think this kind of thing may be the cause of tears, talk to your daughter's key worker. She will want to know, because, just like you, she wants your toddler to feel settled, secure and happy.

## What you can do at home

Nursery is a big change for your toddler and she needs reassurance to feel secure. It's a time when established family routines are particularly important, so avoid major changes at home while she's making this big transition in her life. On the days that she goes to nursery, give her lots of attention when you get home after picking her up. Enjoy a cuddle, snack and chat. Talk to her about what she has had fun doing before encouraging her to chat about any worries. Make sure you acknowledge her feelings. If she expresses concern about something, don't say: 'There's nothing to worry about.' Instead, say: 'I understand, I would feel like that if it happened to me too.' Talking about anxieties will help make them seem less overwhelming. You can also ask her to draw pictures to help her explain. She may find this easier than finding words. If she's worried about making new friends, for example, take action to help her form friendships. Arrange for her to have a playdate with one of the children at the nursery, and involve her by letting her choose who to invite and what they can have for tea.

## A useful challenge

Going to nursery is a big adventure for your toddler. She'll benefit in lots of ways through spending time with other adults and children. She'll develop confidence and communication and social skills. The nursery door may be a challenge now – but rising to the challenge and coming through it will help you both grow stronger. Overcoming separation anxiety now will also prepare your child for later on when she starts school.

# Nursery door routine

Speak to your toddler's key worker and agree a specific routine that you will both stick to when you leave. Here are some ideas:

- Leave home 10 minutes earlier than you would normally, to avoid a rush. Time pressure is stressful for both of you.
- Talk to your toddler about one specific activity she can look forward to at the nursery, such as playing in the sand, cooking or painting.
- Be consistent. Don't say goodbye and leave immediately one day, but hang around for 10 minutes the next. Your toddler needs to know what is going to happen.
- Avoid questions like 'Can I leave you now?' and give clear directions; 'It's time for you to go in and have fun now.'
- Avoid saying: 'I will really miss you' and say instead: 'I'm really looking forward to picking you up this evening.'
- Let her take a favourite teddy with her to reassure her.
- When it is time to leave, take a deep breath and leave. Encourage her key worker to distract her as you go.
- Feel good not guilty; your toddler is in excellent hands, so picture her laughing and enjoying her morning, rather than crying because she wants you.

*Condensed idea*
## Routine and reassurance will soon stop tears at the nursery drop-off

# ⑲ Biting and fighting

Even nice children develop some nasty habits, such as kicking or biting. This might horrify you, but it is unlikely that your toddler will understand what all the fuss is about. It is usually not premeditated or spiteful, but it is important to put a stop to it early on.

## A tricky phase

Many mums and dads say that when their toddler bites another child, it is one of their lowest parenting moments – worse even than a full meltdown in public. Your child may suddenly bite a sibling or a child at nursery. He may even bite people he doesn't know. One of the main reasons why it's tough to remain calm and in control is because of the reaction of other parents who witness the event. They're likely to be shocked and pull their children away, which makes you feel terrible.

However, it may be some consolation to know that you're not alone in having a child who bites or kicks. Between the ages of two and four, the majority of toddlers will have bitten, kicked or had a fight with another child at some time or another. It is a phase that passes and, with your support, most toddlers will grow out of it quite quickly.

You can help by watching out for aggressive play with toys. If your toddler starts to use Buzz Lightyear to demolish Bob the Builder, then it is a good time to intervene. Stop him and say: 'We want Buzz and Bob to be friends and help each other, not hurt each other.' Demonstrate the toys doing something together as a team. It's also a good idea to limit your toddler's exposure to anything he may see that makes him think that violence

Can't go out in public with Jaws! How will he ever make friends? #homealone

is acceptable – an older sibling's video game for example, or certain programmes on TV. Toy weapons can also encourage violence – there's no need to drive yourself insane getting rid of every Dalek – but just be aware of it and keep an eye on how he's behaving with them.

# Why is he so aggressive?

If your toddler bites other children, bear in mind that it's unlikely to be premeditated. He is probably doing it on impulse because it seems like a good idea at the time. The chances are that your child is lovely and thoughtful in all sorts of ways but he may still have an occasional chew on another child. If so, he's probably not biting to hurt someone, but trying to communicate something – and biting is an effective way of doing it. Tune in to what triggers your toddler's biting and see if you can identify any kind of pattern to the situations or the children he chooses. Toddlers bite for different reasons. He may be biting purely to get you to notice him (there's nothing like taking a chunk out of another child to get mum or dad – and everybody else for that matter – looking at him). Biting makes him instantly the centre of attention, so it is a really powerful tool in your toddler's toolbox. Or, he may fight or bite because he's frustrated. In some way, he's trying to make you understand something and you just don't get it – so radical action is called for. He

# How to deal with biting

The following guidelines will help you to create a list of rules for dealing with your toddler when he gets physical:

- If your toddler tries to bite you, put a part of his body in the way (between your body and his mouth).
- If your toddler bites another child, put yourself between him and the victim. Give more attention to the victim, not the biter.
- If the bite has been provoked by a row over a toy, take the toy away from your toddler.
- Never hit or bite a child who fights or bites. If you do this, you are teaching him that it is acceptable behaviour.
- Remove your toddler from the scene. Explain that biting (or kicking) is not acceptable and explain the effect it has on others. Say: 'We do not bite (or kick). It hurts and it's unkind.'
- Tell your toddler calmly and firmly how you do want him to behave; say something like: 'I want you to play so that both of you can have fun.'
- Give your toddler a warning for a minor nip, or time out (three minutes) for a major incident.
- Give your toddler a practical alternative strategy to fighting and biting. Encourage him to come and find you if he is angry, frustrated or worried about anything, so you can talk it through.

may not want to share a toy or to take turns getting a biscuit. Or it may just be that he is tired or hungry and feeling irritable. Whatever the reason, the bite is one big 'shout' for you and your understanding.

If a toddler feels under threat or overwhelmed (by other children or a situation), his inability to express fear verbally may cause him to bite another child instead, which will certainly get your attention. On the other hand, a toddler may bite because he wants to show you, or other children, that he is in control of a situation. He wants to establish a power-base. It's quite common for younger siblings to bite older brothers and sisters for this reason.

## Look for the warning signs

Wherever possible, take your child away from the situation as soon as you see the warning signs of aggression. If he looks as though he's about to wade in physically with his fists, legs or teeth, distract him with another activity. If he clenches his teeth, assume a bite isn't far behind.

Explain your strategies to other people who look after your toddler and make sure they use them consistently too. If he goes to a childminder or nursery, talk to them to make sure you are all dealing with the problem in the same way. If you miss the warning signs and you find yourself witness to your toddler fighting, kicking or biting, respond quickly but keep calm. Make sure that you focus on your child, not on any other parents around you. It's important to be consistent with your biting (or kicking or hitting) rules. You may not see results overnight, but keep going because you need to be determined and committed to deal with this. If you are at all worried, talk to your health visitor or doctor.

# Condensed idea
## You hold the key to breaking your toddler's nasty physical habits

# (20) Embarrassing habits

'Please take your hands out of your pants!' 'Stop picking your nose!' Do these phrases sound familiar? Children often seem to save their most anti-social behaviour for special moments, like the school play or when visiting grandparents. Here are some easy tactics that can help.

## Part of growing up

Unsavoury toddler habits are all part of growing up. Although it can be very embarrassing for you (especially if other people see it happen and comment), your little one won't understand what all the fuss is about. The chances are, he may not even know he's doing it – he has very different ideas from you about what constitutes antisocial behaviour. Antisocial habits are usually harmless and he'll probably grow out of them anyway, but you may want to speed up the process and teach him how to behave in public, so that he learns what is and isn't acceptable.

## Noses are fascinating

Your toddler is at an age when he's keen to explore his body. To him, poking about in his nose is fascinating, especially when he can dig something out and eat it! A lot of toddlers tend to pick their noses when they are tired or bored. Some toddlers do it when their nose is blocked up and they can feel it getting crusty. Some do it to annoy their parents. If you're with your toddler when he starts nose-picking, the best strategy is to distract him; simply divert his hand and attention to something else. Take his hand gently and remove it from his nose, then give him something else to hold in it – a finger puppet can work wonders for fingers itching to do something.

# Hands down pants

Most toddlers, girls and boys, will play with their private parts at some point. It's natural for toddlers to want to know about all the different bits of their bodies. Give your toddler clear direction and attention when you need him to stop. Rather than using the negative phrase 'Don't put your hands down your pants', for instance, say: 'Keep your hands up here' instead (and demonstrate by waving your hands in the air) 'because there are lots of fun things for them to do.'

## Reacting to bad habits

The way you react to your toddler will have a direct influence on his bad habits and on how long they last.

**Do...**
- distract your toddler so that he focuses his attention on other things and can't use his hands for a more antisocial activity
- give him an alternative option (he can take all his clothes off at home, for example, but not in the playground)
- make sure that you or your partner don't have bad habits of your own – if your toddler sees you picking your nose, he'll consider it an acceptable activity!

**Don't...**
- over-react. Keep calm and consider the best course of action
- give him too much attention. This will only encourage him to repeat the behaviour
- punish or humiliate him – it won't solve the problem

## Running naked

Another common toddler pastime is taking off all their clothes. This is completely natural – toddlers love the sheer sense of freedom. However, you may not want your child to do this anytime or anywhere. If so, set a safe place for him to do this. Say: 'We can take our clothes off at home, where it's nice and warm.' Once he knows he has a specific place where he can do it, he is less likely to want to do it when he's out and about.

## Head banging

When toddlers don't get what they want, it's quite common for them to throw a tantrum that includes banging their heads against the closest wall, table or floor. If this happens, you may be beside yourself worrying that he's going to scramble his brain, while also struggling to cope with the fact that the whole world seems to be looking. It's worth remembering at these times that toddlers don't usually hurt themselves – they aim for high noise and low pain. He won't want to do it for long, but you can end it more quickly by distracting him with an activity that requires lots of movement, such as singing 'Row the boat' or banging a drum.

## Your bad habits

Now may be a good time for you to take a look at any bad habits you may have. You can't really blame your toddler for doing something that you do, so beware of what words you use, for example. If a toddler hears something said in private, he's very likely to repeat it loudly in public. If he says something rude, he has to be repeating something he's heard someone say, so make sure it wasn't you. Remember too that he won't have any idea what the 'rude word' means but can see that it has an impact on you. Say

> Can toddlers get ASBOs for nose picking and flicking? #soembarrassed

clearly: 'I don't want to hear that word,' and give him something specific to do with his voice, such as 'I want to hear you sing a nursery rhyme. Let's think of one.'

## Dealing with the problem

If your child is doing things you really don't want him to do and you have decided to intervene, don't be too hard on him. None of us is perfect. The sooner you help him deal with his antisocial habits, the easier they will be to break. The key here is to be matter-of-fact in your approach because it's important not to over-react. You may be wishing the floor will open up and swallow you if your toddler starts picking his nose, but don't draw too much attention to him as you try to stop him. The basic rule here is to keep your toddler's behaviour in perspective. If he often does one particular thing, think about *when* he does it and what may be causing it. He may be totally unaware that he's doing it. He may be bored or tired, or feeling overwhelmed (this is particularly true of nail-biters). Some toddlers do things because they can see it has a real effect on mum or dad and they instantly become the centre of attention. Understanding what may be causing the problem can help you deal with it.

## Condensed idea
### A toddler's antisocial behaviour is a natural part of growing up

# Are we there yet?

Car journeys can be stressful with a toddler, whether it's the nursery run, shopping or a holiday trip. All it takes is a little extra pressure on the driver – you're running late or you're stuck in traffic – and the tension can cause even the best-behaved toddler to throw a tantrum.

## Your attitude is key

Your toddler's behaviour can easily be affected by your mood, but even though you know this, it's inevitable that at times you're likely to get stressed, particularly on car journeys. Driving the car and paying attention to other drivers while keeping a toddler amused is tough, but if you try to relax, it'll make the journey easier.

One of the main reasons that parents – and their toddlers – feel stressed is that they may have left only 'just enough' time to get somewhere. A few red lights are then all it takes to really knock the timing out, and suddenly you're running late. If you're doing a short, local trip, try leaving home a little earlier instead of at the last minute. If you're going on a longer journey, build in planned stops so that you can all get some fresh air, stretch your legs and go to the toilet. Lots of parents find it easier to make longer trips in the early morning or in the evening because there is less traffic and small children will sleep for a lot of the way.

## Be prepared

Get into a positive frame of mind by cleaning out the car before you start, getting rid of all the child-related junk that can build up. Make sure you have everything you need for the journey, including wet wipes,

drinks, healthy snacks and a change of clothing for your toddler. Put a recent photo of your child in your bag; in the absolutely worst-case scenario – such as losing your child in a crowded area – others will be able to help you find him. Think of your toddler's needs too; let him choose a toy to accompany him on the 'great car adventure' and tell him that he has to make sure his toy is having fun on the journey. That way your toddler will be happily occupied while you drive.

## Take a toddler view

Your toddler's screaming or whingeing may set your nerves on edge, but just mentally slip into his car seat for a moment and you might be able to understand why he's making such a fuss. He's strapped in tightly for what seems a lifetime, when all he wants to do is wander about getting stuck into whatever interesting things life throws his way. To you, his car seat means that he's safe, but to him, it means he's a prisoner.

Your toddler's behaviour will seem harder to cope with in a car because you're in a confined space and your attention needs to be on your driving. He could be tired or hungry or bored, and trying to get your attention

# 10 tips for tantrum-free journeys

If you've got a long car journey coming up, try some of the ideas below:

- Sing a song. Put on a CD or playlist of your toddler's favourite songs and have a fun family sing-along.
- Keep a tray or magnetic board with pictures, numbers or letters to play with in the car.
- Finger puppets are great fun for bored toddlers in the back of cars. Ask him to give them names and tell a story about them.
- Play I-Spot. Give your toddler three things to look out for on the journey and see if he can spot them. These could be things like a green traffic light, a dog or a bike. Or ask your toddler to make up his own list.
- Play 1–2–3. Ask him to look out for particular numbers on the numberplates of cars.
- Let your toddler choose an audio book to listen to. Your local library will have a good selection or you can download one from the Internet.
- Take picture books, pop-up books, activity or sticker books and hand them out judiciously during the trip.
- Invest in a portable DVD player and let your toddler take his favourite DVDs. Some parents want to keep the car a screen-free zone, but for others it's a life-saver.
- Borrow a toy from a friend that your toddler's never seen before. The novelty will help keep him amused.
- Shhhh… Challenge your toddler to stay quiet for 5 minutes without making a sound. Give him an egg timer so he can see how he's doing.

to tell you this – he won't understand why you need to concentrate on something other than him. Perhaps seeing the world through his eyes would help you find that extra bit of patience to deal with him positively.

## Car stickers

Car stickers for good behaviour can work wonders on journeys. Begin by telling your toddler you are going to give him a sticker for behaving well in the car and be specific about what you want him to do. Each time you stop, give him the stickers he has earned and then set a new challenge for the next stage of the journey. Keep the goals simple to achieve and easy to reward. As always, remember that if you want your toddler to behave, it's important that you behave well too. Be a good role model – even when you find other drivers challenging – by always remaining calm and polite. Chat to your toddler, too, whenever you feel you can do so safely.

> The new DVD player in the car was worth every penny.
> #peacefuldriver

## Put on the brakes

If your toddler is throwing a tantrum and you are finding it difficult to calm him down, stop the car and deal with it. Give him a book or toy to distract him or, if you have more than one child in the car and they are arguing, you may find it helps to change the seating arrangements. This is all much more easily and safely done at the road side.

## Condensed idea
### Get the entertainment in place before you set off on a long car journey

It can be great fun going away with your toddler, but it can also be stressful for both of you because toddlers like routine – unfamiliarity can bring about challenging behaviour and tantrums. If you're prepared, however, you are more likely to handle them better.

## Where's my routine?

Family life with a toddler is exciting and demanding, and family breaks are no exception. There's no such thing as the 'perfect' family holiday so be realistic about your expectations and recognize that spending a lot of time together in a confined space can put pressure on all of you. Try to understand what may be causing any tantrums that arise and you'll be better equipped to deal with them.

> Need a holiday to recover from this one. #shatteredmum

If your toddler's behaviour is challenging at home, she'll bring that behaviour with her and it may actually get worse. But even if she's fine at home, she may suddenly begin to have tantrums on holiday. This probably isn't because she's being deliberately difficult but because she loves routine and familiarity. You want to get away from it all – but she wants to pack all that familiarity in her suitcase and bring it with her.

It's common for a toddler who has a good evening routine at home to feel overwhelmed by the new experiences and different daily life of being on holiday. Any tantrums in this situation are a call for reassurance. You can understand why: she's away from the security of her own bed and mealtimes may differ from at home. Everything's different! So keep in place as many of the key elements of her routine as you can; like a snuggle and story before bed. Make sure she's packed her favourite teddy and bring a night light if there's room. And be sure she knows you are close by, as this will help her to feel as secure and settled as possible.

# Stress-free days out

If you decide to stay at home for the holidays and have some great days out instead, here are some definite dos and don'ts to consider:

**Do...**
- de-clutter your toddler-bag and take a light pushchair for your little one for when she's tired
- carry out some research. Decide what you really want out of this excursion and what facilities are essential
- book anything you can in advance
- build in regular physical exercise and offer your toddler water and healthy snacks throughout the day

**Don't...**
- rush around trying to pack in as much as you can. Slow down and enjoy what you are doing
- feel you have to go it alone. Plan days out with other parents so you can support each other
- ignore signs of boredom, tiredness or hunger in your toddler. Act before a full-blown tantrum develops
- be afraid to say 'No'. Avoid putting yourself under time or financial pressure by saying 'Yes' to everything

# The food tastes weird

The frantic pace of life means that many families rarely sit down and eat together. So when you're on holiday, make the most of special leisurely family mealtimes. Whether your toddler is a good eater or going through a picky phase, it is not uncommon for children to find strange foods hard to swallow. While it's great to encourage your little one to try new tastes, don't be annoyed if she refuses; it may not be that she's being fussy, it could be because she really doesn't like it. Toddlers need time to get used to new tastes, so if she doesn't want to experiment, don't make her.

# Getting there

Travelling by plane can be an exciting or a scary experience for a little one, or even a little of both. Your toddler will be watching you closely to follow your lead, so if you are worried, she's likely to start worrying too. So make sure she's sitting next to the most relaxed person in your party.

Taking a toddler on a flight can be challenging because it disrupts her daily routine in lots of ways, but there are lots of practical ways you can help her arrive at her destination without going into meltdown. First, be prepared. Make sure you have plenty of wet wipes, nappies, nappy sacks and a change of clothing. Carry a good supply of non-messy snacks, such as breadsticks, and a refillable beaker that won't spill even on the bumpiest flight.

You may want to sit back and relax, but it's better to be realistic and accept that you are your toddler's 'in-flight' entertainer, so come equipped. Ask your child to bring a favourite teddy or doll on to the plane, and encourage her to spend time (and energy) making sure the toy is happy. Take photos of them together – you can ask your child to take some too – to put into a holiday scrapbook when you return. New toys and books can help fend off boredom, and magnetic games really come into their own on plane journeys.

## Create a memory that will last forever

When your toddler is somewhere new, it's very likely that she'll become over-excited at times. While this can be difficult to deal with, especially when you're on holiday, don't be unrealistic in your expectations. You may have told her a dozen times not to run around and get sand over everything, but if you were her age, let loose on a beach, you'd probably be doing exactly the same. So instead of feeling frazzled by flying sand, get stuck in with a bucket and spade, take her to look for crabs or go for a dip in the sea. Spend time, not money, and have fun together on holiday. When you return home, put one of your fun photos somewhere very visible. It's a permanent reminder of what being a family is all about.

## Condensed idea
### Step into your toddler's flip-flops to understand holiday tantrums

# (23) Only mum will do

Your toddler may begin to make it very clear that 'only mum will do' by having a tantrum whenever dad tries to get a look in. In this situation, mum is on call 24/7. It's a normal phase that will pass, but in the meantime here are some tips to help dad share the limelight.

## Toddlers love routine

Generally, toddlers spend more time with one parent than another and so they tend to develop a closer bond with that parent. In many cases it's mum who fulfils this role, and it can be harder for dad to build such a close relationship. Where mum is the primary caregiver, her routines will provide the toddler's life with structure and help him feel secure. So when mum says, 'Dad will give you a bath tonight,' it can send that same, secure toddler into a spin. Why can't mum do it? What's changed? Will dad do it right? It takes a toddler time to get used to any idea that is different – he's not rejecting dad, he's just saying 'I like it the way we usually do it.' He may also be taking the opportunity to show you that he wants to make choices of his own.

> Taking Max to see the movie he's been talking about for weeks, but he's still complaining! What do I need to do? #desperatedad

The way to help your toddler get over this is to give dad regular things to do. That way he becomes part of the regular routine. Identify some practical activities that can be dad's responsibility. Mums need to avoid giving a toddler a choice by saying, 'Would you like dad to read to you tonight?' and instead give clear, confident direction: 'Dad is going to read to you tonight' or 'It's Dad's turn to bath you tonight.' Neither parent should make a big thing about it, but be very matter-of-fact. Your toddler needs to know this is non-negotiable and it is going to happen.

## Be decisive

When toddlers are going to spend time with their dads, it's usually much easier for everyone if mum is out of sight and so isn't an option. Dads and toddlers need to be alone with each other for short periods of time very regularly – just half an hour will make a difference. It's a chance for dad and child to bond, and gives mum a bit of a break. There may be tears when your toddler wants mum and realizes that he isn't going to get his own way, but persevere. Mums need to resist the temptation to step in right away and react to his demands. If your toddler senses mum is weakening, he will carry on making a fuss until he gets what he wants. If he knows mum and dad both mean business, he will begin to get used to the idea, and before long he'll be

looking forward to doing things with dad as well as with mum. It's very important to be consistent; sometimes parents give in because they are tired and aren't feeling strong enough to deal with the tantrum. This may work in the short-term, but in the longer term you will be making life more difficult for yourselves.

# Top tips for rejected dads

If you're being rejected, it's hard not to take it personally and feel offended. It's particularly tough if your little one screams 'Mummy do it' in front of an audience, but try these coping tips:

- Try not to take it personally. This isn't about you and your parenting skills.
- If you're on the end of your toddler's rejection, don't make negative, personal remarks such as, 'You are really upsetting me' or 'Don't say that, it upsets me'.
- Act your age, not his. This is a normal phase that most toddlers go through. If you get upset, your toddler will cling to mum even more.
- Be positive. Give your toddler lots of praise when you do things together. Tell him what you love about being his dad and spending time with him.
- Remember, your confidence may have taken a knock, but it's tough for mum too. If your toddler doesn't want anybody else to do anything, it puts her under pressure. You're a team and together you are stronger. Talk to each other about what is happening and how you want to deal with it. Develop a strategy and make it work.

In addition to involving dad in some of the family routines at home, like bathtime or stories before bed, identify some fun activities as dad's responsibility too. Choose some of your toddler's favourite activities. If your toddler loves swimming, for example, that could become something toddler and dad do in their special one-to-one time. Also consider starting your toddler on some new activity that is special because he does it with his dad. Before long, something like going to the soft-play park together on a Saturday morning or jumping over puddles together will become a family tradition.

## Widen the circle

If only mum will do, it's not only dad who gets rejected. Your toddler will try the same tactic on trusted friends and relatives. There are lots of good reasons for getting your toddler used to doing things with other adults, not just mum and dad. It's good for the development of your little one's confidence and his social and communication skills. It also gives parents a break and it means friends and family can really feel involved in your toddler's life.

The easiest way to establish this is to leave your toddler with friends and family for short, regular lengths of time. He will soon get used to being with them and they'll find all sorts of new and interesting ways to enjoy each other's company. Also try taking your toddler to places where he will naturally come into contact with different adults that he trusts (such as playgroup), so that he gets used to the idea of being around different adults and knows he can approach them for help, if he needs to. If your toddler really clings to mum, try diverting his attention to a fun activity – this may be enough to take his mind and arms elsewhere.

## Condensed idea
### If you feel rejected as a dad, spend more time – not less – with your toddler

# (24) She prefers the nanny!

There may come a day when your toddler makes it clear she prefers her childminder or nanny to you. This is an issue that affects working parents in particular. It's natural to feel hurt and guilty when this happens, but remind yourself that it is only temporary and it will pass.

## Toddlers have phases

If both parents go out to work and leave their toddler with a childminder or nanny, that person will be spending a lot of time with the child. In this situation, it's totally normal for a little one to prefer the caregiver from time to time. Toddlers love routine, and if the parent who normally does the lion's share of the caring can no longer be at home for several days a week, your toddler will (sensibly) begin to get used to someone else playing with her, feeding her and looking after her. Once you recognize this and understand that this is an entirely natural toddler reaction, it may help you to deal with your feelings, should this happen to you. Instead of seeing it negatively and getting upset by it, try to take a positive perspective and make good use of the time that you've freed up. For example, you can relax on evenings out knowing that if your toddler wakes up, she will feel entirely comfortable with her carer, who will be able to get her back to sleep.

No one can ever usurp a parent's special role, so don't start worrying that you're no longer important to your little one. All toddlers go through phases of having a favourite and, while it's hard to endure at the time, the phases always pass. Just remember that childminders will come and go, but you will always be your toddler's mum or dad and you are in a lifelong relationship with her.

Be aware of your feelings, and make sure you don't react negatively in front of your toddler if she reaches for a childminder instead of you. Try not to show your toddler that you are upset because this will upset her too, especially if she thinks it is because of something she said or did. When she clings on to her childminder and doesn't want to come to you, do everything you can to keep calm and smiling.

# Dr Jekyll and Mr Hyde

As well as coping with the feelings of being rejected by your toddler, it's common for parents to find that their toddlers will behave like angels for other adults – but not for them. If so, remember the following points:

- Toddler tantrums are common after a day with a childminder. Your little one's been trying hard to hold everything together – and lets it all out in the comfort of her own home.
- You're often on the sharp end of challenging behaviour because your toddler craves your attention. But don't be tempted to forget boundaries and let her get away with things you wouldn't normally allow, just because you've been at work all day.
- Have a plan. If she starts to scream, say: 'I am going to build a tower with your blocks and, if you want to, you can come and play with me.' Then do it. She'll soon decide that playing is more fun that having a tantrum.
- Take heart. It's a sign you have a really strong relationship. She knows that you are her mum, that you love her and will always be there for her, regardless of how she behaves. She may not be quite so sure of this when it comes to other adults.

# It's good to love other people

It may not seem it at the moment, but actually you are in a good position. You've made a great decision and chosen a childminder you and your toddler both really like. This is really good news for both of you – you don't want your toddler to be crying for you all of the time that you are away from her. You know that when you are away from your toddler she is with someone she loves and has fun with. We all want to feel wanted, but there are real advantages to your childminder being the flavour of the month.

Take a look at your toddler and consider that what this also means is that she's confident and can communicate and establish relationships with other adults. She's developing great social and communication skills which will make it easier for her to develop new relationships with other adults at nursery or school and in a wide range of social situations.

> I'm no longer the hand that rocks the cradle! #workingmum

It's actually a good idea to get into the habit of praising your childminder, because your child needs to know that she's in safe, trusted hands. It's also important to recognize that the negative feelings you have about the situation are about you – not about the carer. You may be feeling vulnerable and wondering whether your relationship with your toddler is being undermined, but this is your fear, not the real situation. Let go of the guilt, recognize that it's good for your child to be with someone she loves, and remind yourself that your childminder is doing nothing to bring on these feelings – she's just doing a great job.

# Leave work on time

There are always good reasons to stay at work, but focus instead on the excellent reason to leave on time: you're going home to be a mum. If you're rushing from work to the childminder's you may arrive feeling tense, which in turn could make your childminder and your toddler feel tense. Arrive looking forward to seeing your toddler and spending one-to-one time with her when you get home. Toddlers don't like transitions, so give her warning she is going to leave: 'You can draw one more shape and then we are going.' Agree an exit strategy with your childminder so that it is the same every day. You can involve your toddler too with questions like, 'Do you want to put on your shoes first or your coat?' If your toddler feels involved in the routine, she'll be much more likely to leave happily and quietly.

If your childminder has established routines with your toddler, focus on what habitual things you and your little one can do together. It may be a game of 'tickle monsters' you play when you get home, or a special book you read together after bathtime. Choose something that you both enjoy and which will help you build an even better connection with your toddler. Your time together may be limited, so make sure you enjoy it and can be 100 per cent with your child. Parents tend to be the ones who do routine things while other people (like grandparents) do the fun and exciting things. So make sure that you and your toddler get 'fun time' too!

## Condensed idea
### Your toddler will always love you more than everyone else, no matter what she says or does

When your toddler starts nursery, his social life really takes off. He'll probably be more in demand than you are, with a party invitation or playdate every week. However, not all toddlers will mix with other children when they're out, even if they are sociable at home.

## Every toddler is different

Some toddlers make socializing look easy. They can work the room like a seasoned professional – laughing, chatting and giving high-fives. But for lots of toddlers, mixing with other children and adults can be overwhelming. If your toddler prefers his own company, he may behave

in a range of different ways. He may cling to you or another adult; he may sit on his own, not talking to anyone but watching everything that is going on; or he may be totally disengaged, not making contact, sitting with his back to the room. If he does say anything to the other toddlers around him,

> **Sam wants to be friendly, but he's so shy. Dad to the rescue with party games!** #socialwhirl

his nerves may get the better of him and he may be hard to understand. Recognize that your little one is not behaving badly – he's struggling to get to grips with a big new social world.

It is natural for you to want your child to be a good socializer. You want to see him enjoying being with other children, playing well together and having fun. But the reality is that it takes little ones time to deal with situations they find daunting and time to develop the confidence and social skills they need. There's no 'one shoe fits all' approach here: you need to develop a tailor-made strategy that suits your child.

## Relax and be sociable yourself

If you take your toddler to a child's birthday party, or to his playgroup, and you're feeling tense because you are anticipating how he may behave, your toddler will feel tense too. So relax and think positive. Enlist the help of another mum or dad whose child is going to the same event, as you, and go along all together so that your toddler arrives with a friend. This will give him a bit of extra confidence.

The best thing you can do to help him is to take a look at your own behaviour and check to see that you're making a real effort to mix with other parents. If he sees you chatting to parents and children you don't know very well, he is much more likely to do the same. So make mixing with other parents a real priority – start a conversation, whether you're at a party, at the nursery, in the park or at the supermarket checkout.

# From shy to sociable

It's very common for toddlers to be shy. It may take your little
one time to have confidence in social situations but there are lots
of things you can do to build his self-esteem and help him feel
comfortable in a crowd:

- Get down to his level and practise eye-to-eye contact. Be very
  positive and enthusiastic every time he engages with you. Say to
  him, 'I love to see your smiley eyes,' and get friends and family
  to do the same with him.
- Organize regular playdates with other toddlers at your home
  so he can get comfortable with socializing there first. Start with
  one other toddler and then gradually introduce a few more, so
  that he gets used to being with a circle of friends, not just one.
- Prepare him for going to a party. Tell him who is going and
  explain what is going to happen. Toddlers don't like surprises.
- Help your toddler to mix by doing it together. Instead of saying
  to him, 'Go and play with Rafferty,' say, 'Come on, Rafferty looks
  as though he's having fun – let's go and see what he's up to.' If
  he finds a social situation overwhelming, you can help him take
  the first step and this will help him feel secure and confident.
- Family life is about choices, and if your toddler
  finds mixing stressful, you don't have to
  accept every single invitation. Yes, it's good
  for him to have the practice and gradually
  get used to that whole new toddler social
  scene – but take it a step at a time. If you
  do say no to an invitation, be positive about
  it and go and enjoy special one-to-one time
  with your little one instead.

# Don't force it

If your toddler really doesn't want to mix, don't force him to. And if he doesn't want to say hello, don't feel that you have to move heaven and earth to make him, because it's likely to have the reverse affect and also to make him upset. It's best to avoid drawing attention to your toddler's behaviour and making remarks about it, and whatever you do, don't compare his behaviour with that of other children. Your toddler is his own little person. You can't change him – and you wouldn't want to – so let him take socializing at his own pace. He's got plenty of time ahead of him to find his way.

Commit to banishing the word 'shy' from your vocabulary. If you are using the word with your toddler or he hears you telling other parents he is shy, the chances are that he'll become more shy, not less. You may not even mean it as a complaint, but there's a chance that it may come across as something negative to him. The more you talk about it and give it a name, the more he may think that there is something wrong with him. And of course there isn't.

Focus instead on what your toddler does well socially and catch him 'red-handed' mixing successfully with other children. Praise him at the moment he plays well with a friend and be specific about what he is doing that you like by saying: 'It looks like you're having great fun playing with your friends, you're doing a great job sharing your cars with them.' Look out for any small signs of improvement and draw attention to them. He may not be a social butterfly for the entire party, but there will be things he does that show he's starting to move in the right direction – so make sure he knows you've noticed them.

## Condensed idea
## Some toddlers take longer than others to feel comfortable about socializing

# 26 I'm fine on my own

**When your toddler begins to assert her independence, you're likely to hear her saying 'Me do it!' more and more. This vital milestone means she is developing her own identity, and nurturing that independence is one of the most important jobs you'll do as a parent.**

## Defiance is normal

As a baby, your child was totally dependent on you, but now she's a toddler, she's keen to do as much as she can for herself. 'Me' becomes her enthusiastic mantra and, as a parent, it's rewarding to see her wanting to be able to do things on her own. After all, independence is high up on our list of priorities in terms of what we want to teach our children. But those toddler steps towards independence can also be stressful; she's beginning to make her own decisions about what she does and doesn't want to do, and her decisions may not always be the same as yours. The best way to approach your toddler is to expect her to refuse to do what you want and deal with it accordingly – that is absolutely normal at this stage.

> Will seems to have discovered the meaning of willpower!
> #defeateddad

## Avoid ultimatums

When your toddler is determined to demonstrate she has her own mind, it can be very easy to fall into the trap of using threats and ultimatums. But try to avoid this (or engaging in any kind of power struggle) as it will

# Six ways to nurture independence

The best way to encourage your toddler to be independent is to love her unconditionally, be supportive and have bags of patience. Here are six practical ideas to try that will help you both:

- If your toddler can do it then let her do it. It's going to take longer for her to feed herself, dress herself or brush her own hair, so allow a bit of extra time. If she's struggling, resist the temptation to take over and give her practical advice instead.
- Believe in her. Often just saying, 'You can do it!' will help give her the confidence to believe she can – and she will.
- Help her to explore her world. Encourage her to be curious and to ask lots of questions. Make your home as toddler-proof as possible so that she can explore safely without you constantly saying, 'No, don't touch that.'
- Mix with others frequently. Get your toddler used to spending time with other adults and children. Include times when you are away from her for short periods of time so she learns to stand on her own two feet.
- Encourage choice and me-time. Let her choose what fruit to eat or what shoes to wear, what books to read or games to play, and encourage her to learn to play by herself for short periods of time.
- Try new things together. Encourage your toddler to step outside her comfort zone. If, for example, she is hesitant about getting onto a see-saw at the park, stand behind her and hold her so that she knows she is safe. She needs to know that you are there and when she is confident, she'll do it alone.

Encourage your toddler to explore by giving her treasure maps for objects hidden around the home. Snacks and a drink are essential provisions!

make her feel as though she's being forced into a corner, with only two choices: either to do something she really doesn't want to do, or to suffer whatever you're threatening. It's all about control, and she's at a stage now where she doesn't want you to be controlling her. She wants to get herself dressed, feed herself and make decisions about how she spends her time. As a result, her behaviour may come across as defiant, and that can be exasperating – but remember that she's going through a confusing time. So when she refuses to get dressed, instead of saying, 'If you don't get dressed right now, I am going to…' say, 'When you get dressed, we can go to nursery. Do you want to wear pink tights or blue ones?'

## Get cooking

Often, as parents, we do housework and chores ourselves because they have to be done and it's easier and quicker to do them alone. This is true in the shortterm but definitely not in the longterm. The thing is, if we do everything for our children when they are young, what happens when they leave home? We want to prepare them to be able to look after themselves and this is the perfect time to start. We may dread household chores, but toddlers love to help and our boring chores become their exciting challenges. So let her beat eggs, pour milk into a bowl, set the table, move laundry, dust and sort things out for you. Sharing the load is good for us – and it's great for a toddler's sense of independence. She's little now, but helping to cut bananas with a plastic knife may be the first step towards her being able to help you cook healthy meals for the family when she's older.

## Follow your toddler's lead

This is an exciting and sometimes overwhelming time for your toddler. You may notice she has rapid mood changes – wanting to be independent one moment and stuck like Velcro to your side the next. The best way to handle this is to follow your toddler's lead; if she wants to do things her own way and it's possible, let her; if she wants to cling to you, let her know that's fine as well. Above all, be flexible – this is easier for you, as the adult, than it is for her.

Nurturing your child's independence is like letting go with elastic. It takes time and energy to get the balance right: sometimes you'll think she wants to be at a distance from you, out there on her own and doing her own thing, then suddenly she'll come bouncing back for support and reassurance before she starts stepping out again. Think of this time as good practice for when she's a teenager, wavering in much the same way between being a child (dependent) and an adult (independent). Your role is to be there, 'on call', to lend the support she needs.

## Condensed idea
### Learning to be independent doesn't have to be stressful for toddlers or their parents

# (27) I'm okay, you're okay

You want your toddler to believe in himself and to go out into the world with the confidence to enjoy life's adventures. You want him to be who he wants to be and love every minute of it. These tips will show you how to boost his confidence and avoid crushing it.

## Building self-belief

Self-belief and confidence are the most valuable gifts you can give your child. With self-belief your toddler will feel valued and good about himself. He'll believe he can achieve what he sets out to do and won't be afraid to keep on trying, even if things don't work out the way he wanted them to.

> Joe thinks there's no such word as can't. He's right! #suredad

If your toddler grows up feeling confident about himself, he will see the world as being one with plenty of exciting opportunities and he won't be afraid to try new challenges. If you teach your toddler to believe that he can do anything he sets out to do – he probably will. And, conversely, if he grows up believing he's not capable of doing things – he'll be absolutely right. He won't. Having the right frame of mind is half the battle, and it's an important lesson to teach your toddler.

As your toddler grows, he will begin to understand more and more about himself. He's just beginning to realize that he's a person in his own right with his own identity and very definitely a mind of his own. Some of his more challenging behaviour will occur as a result of this new-found wisdom, as he tries to work out where the boundaries are.

# Outer confidence

Your toddler will develop two kinds of confidence: outer and inner confidence. His outer confidence will come from the messages he gets from you. You can boost this by spending time with him; knowing you want to be with him will help him feel valued. Telling him you love him, what you love about being his mum or dad and spending time with him will all help strengthen his belief in himself. Give specific examples, such as: 'I loved making lunch with you because we had so much fun making the fruit into funny faces.' Show him lots of affection, too, with loads of kisses and cuddles. Toddlers believe that everything you say is true, so be careful never to label him in a negative way; this can really knock his confidence. Talk about his behaviour not him. Instead of saying, 'You're unkind,' say, 'It is unkind to hit your sister.' It is his behaviour that is the issue, not 'he' himself, and his behaviour happens at a particular moment in time. It is also something he can change. But if he believes that he is fundamentally unkind, silly or wrong – as a person – it may begin to have negative implications and affect his confidence in himself.

# Inner confidence

Your toddler's inner confidence is dependent on what he thinks and says about himself. You can boost this by helping him talk about his feelings and particularly what he enjoys doing. When he has painted a picture, encourage him to say what he likes about it. The more he talks, the stronger the positive feeling will become and he will think 'Yes, I can paint!' It's important, too, to challenge any limiting beliefs that he has about himself. If, for example, he says 'I can't do it' when he's trying to put on a shoe, say, 'You can't do it *yet* but you will be able to soon.' The word 'yet' is a very powerful one and sends him the message that what is tough at the moment will be possible in the future.

## Work in small chunks

Get into the habit of breaking down toddler-tasks into small manageable steps that your little one can manage. Instead of saying, 'Put your shoes and socks on,' say, 'Can you put your socks on first? Good! You've done it. Now can you find the right shoe for this foot?' Each little step that your toddler completes will be a boost to his confidence. Set aside time at the weekend to teach your toddler a basic skill such as doing up shoes, so that you have ample (and relaxed) time to help him – rather than trying to do it as you're rushing out through the door. Praise him as each step is completed and encourage him to say, 'I can.'

## Forget about failure

Your toddler learns about life from you. If you judge your life in terms of success and failure, he'll learn to do that too. Get out of the habit of using the word 'fail' and treat everything as an experience you can learn from, such as telling yourself (and your toddler), 'I've tried it this way and it didn't work so now I'll try something else instead.' If that's how you talk about a work problem or making a cake, your toddler will take the same approach to building a model or doing a jigsaw, and the word 'fail' won't enter his head. By giving your little one lots of learning opportunities, support and love, you'll see his confidence grow and grow as he masters different skills. Later on, when he's facing a challenge he hasn't tried before, instead of being afraid to try, he will have the confidence to rise to the challenge – even if you are not by his side – and have a go. He'll have mastered a vital life skill.

# Confidence crushers and boosters

Every day is an opportunity to nurture your toddler's confidence. Here are five tips for you to try and five things to avoid:

### Confidence boosters
- Listen more than you talk – you have two ears and one mouth for a reason.
- Praise your toddler for having a go, not just for succeeding.
- Stick your toddler's pictures up on the fridge and find a special space in the house to display his toddler creations.
- Encourage him to try lots of different activities and he'll find lots of things he's good at.
- Get down to his level and have fun together. Show him you love spending time with him.

### Confidence crushers
- Don't make comparisons between your toddler and another.
- Don't talk more about what he does wrong than he does well.
- Don't compare your child to a mythical 'perfect child'. If your toddler feels he's less than perfect to you, he'll feel inadequate. Enjoy having your unique, imperfect toddler.
- Don't rush in and take over when he wants to try for himself.

## Condensed idea
### Boost your toddler's confidence with love and positivity

# (28) Be positive, not pushy

You want your toddler to achieve her potential and get a great start in life. But how do you know when you're stepping over the line and morphing from a positive parent into a pushy one? Here are some warning signs to look out for and advice to keep you on the right track.

## Too much on the calendar?

Most parents want to do everything they possibly can for their children. This often includes making as many activities available as possible – encouraging her to have a wide range of diverse experiences. That's a great goal to aim for, but how can you make sure that you get the balance right and don't fall into the trap of putting your child under too much pressure? It's surprisingly easy to find yourself wanting your child to

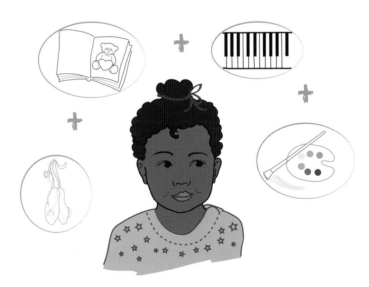

achieve what *you* want her to achieve, rather than what she is ready for. Asking too much too soon from your toddler could have the opposite effect and put her off altogether. The answer is to go with your gut instinct, because it will be right. Whenever you are thinking of scheduling something into your toddler's calendar, make sure that it feels right to do so. If your heart

> Is yoga, music class and swimming too much in one toddler day? #busyparent

says yes, go with it; but if your heart says no, or even 'Is this too much?', stop and think for a second. Chances are there's enough in her schedule already and you already know that one extra thing will be one activity too many. Trust your instincts – you'll get a recognizable feeling for when you are starting to push her beyond a comfortable level.

## Don't get competitive

All toddlers develop at different times and at varying rates, so the only benchmark that is important is your toddler – not anyone else. This holds true whether the issue is potty training, socializing, eating or talking. The challenge comes when mums and dads start talking about what their children can and can't do, and you find yourself comparing this with what your toddler can do. It's easy to find yourself suddenly feeling very competitive, especially when other parents ask things like 'Is she dry yet? Does she always eat vegetables? When do you think she'll be able to say "banana"?' Rather than getting into a verbal sparring match about exactly where each toddler is in a particular aspect of their development, switch the conversation to a more positive direction instead. Talk about what the children *enjoy* doing, rather than what they are good at doing, so you can stop worrying and start celebrating your toddler's activities.

It's great to have support from other parents. There are times when they are a lifeline and you may turn to them for advice, reassurance and cups

# Let your toddler set the pace

The best way to support your toddler is to always make sure that you are going at her speed – not yours or any other parents:

- Focus on activities she does well and enjoys and this will give her confidence with activities she finds more challenging.
- Celebrate what your toddler can do, not what she can't.
- Be realistic about what you are asking your toddler to achieve. Then break it down into small steps, and she will succeed.
- Praise her when she has a go and shows effort and determination – not just when she achieves something.
- Never say, 'So-and-so can do this, so you can too.'
- Don't live your life through her – just because you loved doing gymnastics or playing the piano doesn't mean she will too.
- Never say 'I've showed you how to do that 100 times…!' because it isn't true, although it may feel like it. Remember, too, that toddlers need repetition after repetition in order to learn.
- Give her some choice in what she does. Even if all her friends love ballet, it doesn't mean that she has to do ballet too.
- Don't try to force her into doing something she doesn't want to do – it may put her off altogether.

of tea. But don't fall into the trap of comparing what your toddler can do physically, emotionally or socially with what their toddler is capable of. Your child is a unique little person, travelling along life's motorway at her own speed (sometimes even parking up on the hard shoulder for a while). As long as she is happy, confident and generally heading in the right direction, you can relax and be happy.

# Downtime is just as important

These days it can be hard to choose between the myriad activities on offer for toddlers and it's tempting to pack as much as possible into every waking hour. But being a toddler takes lots of energy and, just like you, she needs to re-charge her batteries, so be sure to give yourself and your toddler time to relax. It's also important for both of you to have one-to-one time together. Bonding takes time – it's not something to squeeze in between toddler gym and yet another playdate. It's worth remembering that if you gave your toddler the choice, she would choose spending time with you alone over any of the activities that you have lined up for her.

# Making choices

When you're in a group of parents all signing their toddlers up for their fifth activity of the week, it can be tempting to follow the crowd, because you don't want yours to be 'missing out'. If you ever have this feeling, remember that no child can do literally everything on offer, so you need to prioritize what you want her to do. There's no denying that it's good for your toddler to have lots of experiences, but it's also good for her to learn that life is about choices and priorities. Bear in mind, too, that toddlers don't have a clear idea of what kind of activity they will like, so make sure she knows that it's fine for her to give up if she isn't enjoying it. Giving up on something now doesn't mean she'll constantly be handing in her notice when she's an adult. When she says she wants to stop, all she's saying is 'I'm not having fun', so rather than force her to carry on, let her keep her options open and tell her that she can try again another day.

## Condensed idea
### The most important thing – time with you alone – doesn't appear on anyone else's schedule

# Family values

Having a child offers a great opportunity to take a fresh look at what's important to you when it comes to the way you live your life. Your values make you who you are, so it's important that they feel right and that you're happy to pass them on to your child.

## Values give you direction

Most parents recognize the importance of having good values. Your values are like a compass – they give you direction as you move along on the sea of life. Without values, you'd be bobbing along going this way and that, but never really getting where you want to go. The more you live by your values, the more positive, motivated and happy you will feel – and so will your family. They may be the most important thing to get right – because what your toddler learns from you in this regard will serve as a compass in his life too.

## Practise what you preach

If you didn't give values much concentrated attention or thought when your child was a baby, now is the time to think about them. A survey of 500 parents in 2012 by The Parent Coaching Academy, UK, revealed that the top three values parents want to

> Dad said Liam's a chip off the old block. He should know! #ditto

make sure they pass on are a strong sense of right and wrong, and the importance of love and of honesty. They also say that the values they think their toddlers most enjoy living by are a sense of adventure, fun

# Five ways to show that love matters

For many parents, love is the most important value. On busy days, we may take it for granted that our child knows that he's loved, but this isn't necessarily true, so try these tips to make sure your little one knows how much you love him:

- Find a time every day to tell your toddler what you love about being his mum or dad.
- Give him lots of cuddles and kisses.
- Surprise him – draw a big heart and give it to him and say, 'I love you.' Or put a small heart in his packed lunch so he'll find it at the nursery.
- Don't limit your love to your toddler. Be openly and explicitly affectionate towards your partner.
- Tell your toddler what you love about your mum and dad or friends or relatives. Showing your toddler how to receive love and give it may be the greatest gift you give him.

and security. Every parent is different and while this survey gives an insight into what some parents believe, you will have your own sense of what's important to you and what values you want to live by and pass on to your toddler.

Passing your values on to your toddler takes time. There are certain things you can teach your toddler – but values are really 'caught, not taught'. It is how you live your life that is key. If you are living your values in your daily life – in what you do, not just what you say – he will too. Use examples from daily situations and the books you share together. Children's books are usually strong on values so get your

toddler involved in the story and talk about the parts that point to values that you think are important. For example, ask your toddler what he thinks about the way characters behave, and which of them he would like to have as his friend and why?

## Be honest and praise kindness

If you want your toddler to learn about honesty, you need to be a great role model and demonstrate this consistently – not send a confusing message that sometimes 'white lies' are okay. If you tell a friend your toddler can't go to tea because he's a bit under the weather, when actually it's because you've got too much to do at home, or you say to him, 'Don't tell dad you bought sweets today,' he will learn that it is all right to tell lies in certain situations.

Introducing your values is something you can do on a daily basis. Whenever you're with him, make a point of praising him for kindness and helping others, whether it is helping his baby sister make a jigsaw, or helping you sort out the laundry. Make sure he knows you have noticed and that you really like this behaviour.

Give special attention to any good behaviour your toddler shows without being asked and tell him how good it makes you feel. This is particularly important because he is choosing to do it himself. If you see him sharing a toy with a friend, for example, you could say to him, 'I love seeing you both taking turns with your car. It makes me feel happy'. Your pleasure acts as a reward for him, and he is likely to repeat the behaviour.

## Justice, courage and consideration

Another value that you may think is important is that of justice. If your toddler breaks a friend's toy on purpose, ask him what made him do it. Make sure you listen without judgement, then acknowledge his feelings (it may be because it was bigger or better than his). Explain that it was wrong and encourage him to say sorry and do something to make it up to his friend.

Another value that will help your toddler later in life is courage. You can encourage him to be brave by giving him lots of praise whenever he does something you know is hard for him. If, for example, he joins in a game at the park when you know he'd rather be holding your hand, or he has a go on the big swing for the first time even though he is nervous, say: 'Well done for being so brave. You are a real adventurer.'

Learning to be considerate towards others is another important value to learn. If your toddler is doing something that is upsetting you or another child, talk to him about it calmly and ask him for his ideas about what he can do to behave in a way that will help you or them feel happier. Consideration and empathy don't necessarily come naturally to small children, or to some adults either for that matter!

## Condensed idea
### The values you live by will become your toddler's values

Your toddler is learning to communicate in lots of different ways. She may not always have all the words she wants, but she'll try everything she can to get her message across, and there are lots of practical ways that you can help her during this frustrating time.

## Communicate positively

We all learn to communicate in different ways. Your toddler may be desperate to tell you something but doesn't know how to do it, so the more ways you can show her to get her message across, the more she'll be able to achieve. Probably the most important lesson you can teach your toddler is to communicate positively, by modelling this yourself. If you suffer a kind of irritated meltdown while trying to get your point across to her, and simply tell her to do something, she'll take to communicating with orders too. Show her how to get a message across positively and she will follow your lead – say 'If you hang up your coat, it won't get rumpled,' rather than 'Pick up your coat! How many times do I have to tell you?' Avoid blame, smile more often than you frown, and say 'Yes' more often than 'No'. Be sure, too, that you're saying 'You can!' more often than 'You can't'.

> Four months ago not a peep. Now I can't get a word in edgeways! #chattermatters

Chatter really does matter when it comes to your little one. Your toddler learns about talking and using new words from you, so talk to her often and listen as she talks to you. She'll enjoy hearing her own voice and listening to yours. She will mirror back the things you say and the way you say them (this can be quite disconcerting!). So talk to her as often as possible, as positively as possible, and with a wide range of vocabulary. The more words she hears and tries, the more her confidence and vocabulary will grow. Get down to her level and look at her when you are talking. When you are out and about, get into the habit of describing what you are doing and what you can see and hear and smell. Get into the habit of pointing things out and naming them. Repetition is great for language development, so when you say a new word, let her say it back to you. Talk to her in your normal voice – not in baby talk – and she will learn to talk like that too.

## Encourage talking

If you want your toddler to listen, it's important that you listen to her. So make sure there are times when she has your undivided attention – perhaps at breakfast, after nursery or when you are tucking her into bed. Tell her, 'I'm listening', and maintain eye contact with her as you listen to her chatter. She'll feel loved and important, and will know that what she says is heard and understood.

Your toddler may be happy to practise all the words she's using, or she may still prefer to make noises and point at her juice cup, rather than ask you for a drink. If your child is capable of talking and just doesn't want to play the game, say to her, 'What do you want?' and encourage her to have a go at expressing herself in words. If she still refuses, say what you think she means so that she can hear, such as: 'I want a drink please'. Praise her for talking well and using interesting words. This takes time and effort – but it will definitely help her in the long run.

## Talk with your hands

Sometimes you might want to reinforce a verbal message by accompanying the words with a sign that your toddler can see. For instance, 'Could you please play more quietly?' might be accompanied by putting your finger to your lips. Or you might sign a high-five to show that you think she's trying really hard. Be consistent with the words and signs so she learns them and can use them herself if she is ever struggling to find the right words to communicate something to you.

When you are showing your toddler how to do something, demonstrate it first and explain what you are doing. If you are teaching her how to put on her shoes, for instance, show her how to do it and talk about what you are doing. Then let her have a go by herself.

# Five ways to boost vocabulary

Here are some practical ideas to help you increase your toddler's vocabulary so she has plenty of words at her fingertips.

- Stick labels on objects: make three labels, each showing a word and picture of something (such as a table, teddy and book). Play a game by asking her to try to find each of the objects in the room and put the right labels on them.
- Put on a CD of one of your toddler's favourite stories and listen to it together.
- Sing songs and nursery rhymes together and do the actions to accompany the words you are singing.
- Enjoy sharing books together. In addition to reading the words, point out all the different things in the pictures. Play a game with her, asking questions such as 'Can you show me the sun?' and 'Where is the teddy?'
- Let your toddler practise her talking and listening skills in the company of a range of other adults and children.

If your toddler is struggling to find the right words and begins to get frustrated, say to her, 'Show me' and teach her to take your hand and take you to the teddy or the book that she wants you to see. This lets her know you want to help. You can also use pictures to show her what you want her to do in her morning or evening routines, so that she has a visual map as well as your verbal instructions.

## Draw it

Every toddler is a budding artist, so tap into this – you can both use drawing as a way to communicate. This can be particularly helpful when she's trying to describe things that you haven't seen yourself – such as what she did at her aunt's house or who her friends are at nursery. Put up the pictures you and your toddler draw around your home and make a point of using them to stimulate conversation in lots of different ways. When you're having a quiet hour or so together, ask her to draw pictures for you sometimes, and then ask her questions so that she can talk to you about them. Take inspiration from everything around you as starting points for a good chat.

## Condensed idea
### Toddlers learn to talk through talking and listening, so you need to talk and listen too

# 31 Fun, not frantic

With a toddler, it's non-stop from the moment he wakes up and despite wanting to be a fun parent, you probably feel as though you end up being frantic instead. Creating time for you and your toddler to play together is essential for his wellbeing and development – and yours.

## Fun families

If you're a frantic parent, rushing around from one thing to the next, your toddler will grow up in that kind of world and assume it's normal. Fun parents, on the other hand, have fun toddlers and create some really great memories for their children. Your child certainly won't remember the hours you spent vacuuming the house or doing the weekly shop – but

> Can't stop to talk. Too busy ferrying toddler to clubs and sports lessons. Is this right? #24/7mum

he will remember the times you made pancakes or raced twigs down a stream. Fun families are healthy families: research shows that the more you laugh, the longer you are likely to live.

Before you had children you were probably all set on being a fun parent. But the reality is very different, mainly because whether you're a stay-at-home parent or juggling home life with a job, you'll feel as though you're working 24 hours a day. The early years of parenting can be incredibly tough. You're likely to have 101 things going through your mind: mainly things to do, find and make happen. Most parents say that even when they are playing with their toddler they can't stop all sorts of other things whizzing through their mind, and that is absolutely normal. However, while you're scheduling lots of activities for your toddler, remember that playing isn't something to fit in between other more pressing activities – it is essential for his physical, emotional and social wellbeing and development. It's through play that your toddler will learn about himself, his family and the world he lives in.

Toddlers are mini-scientists, testing out their hypotheses about the world, and they use all of their senses to do this. You'll see your child smelling, touching, seeing, squeezing – and throwing just about everything. That's because he's wondering how fast something can fly and how quickly it falls. He'll put things inside one another, because he knows he can fit in a supermarket trolley, but can he fit in a cardboard box? You'll see his play become increasingly imaginative, demonstrating his creative problem-solving skills. Playing is a very positive channel for a toddler's energy and enthusiasm, and, because he's enjoying himself, his behaviour will be at its best. So there are lots of great reasons to prioritize play sessions.

# Fun tips for parents

Every toddler is different, so work out what things your child loves doing and find ways to slot them into your week. Here are some simple ideas to get you started and boost your fun factor:

- Do more of the things that make you both laugh.
- Remember that you are your toddler's most important toy: be available for having fun.
- Be unpredictable. Do something fun that surprises him, like having a go on his scooter.
- Draw faces on the soles of each other's feet.
- Help him create a car or a rocket from a big cardboard box and travel with him around your home.
- Get outside and into the fresh air. Take a ball to throw or kick, roll down a hill or hold his hand and run down as fast as you can.
- Get into role playing. Toddlers love to play teachers, mums, dads and doctors. Get your first aid kit out, for instance, and turn his bedroom into a toy hospital.
- Act out his favourite books together.
- Learn to take mess in your stride. A messy home is a fun, family home.

## Learn from your toddler

Your toddler is an absolute expert at enjoying himself. He knows what he likes and what he wants, and he has an absolute determination to make sure that no one gets in his way. He's definitely got the fun factor. Parents find it hard to 'live in the moment' – a skill much praised by Buddhists – but toddlers do this naturally most of the time and it's something that parents could benefit from learning, too.

# Put it in the diary

Parents are great time managers. They are practical problem-solvers and they get things done. So once you prioritize being fun, not frantic, realize that you are in control of the schedule and can make it happen. Decide today that you're going to take control of your time and make 'living in the moment' a priority. If it helps, put it in the diary so that you make sure you have time put aside and it doesn't clash with any of those 'must do' jobs. By allowing play time for you and your toddler together, you will be making sure your toddler doesn't grow up in a world where life is just one long deadline.

There's no magic wand you can wave to guarantee that while the two of you are playing, you won't think about chores that need doing or other things that make you feel under pressure. But a great first step is to stop worrying about what you *have* to do and start looking forward to what you *want* to do. And luckily your toddler is an expert in that way of thinking. If you decide you are going to have fun, you will, and you'll be a fun parent. So relax and enjoy yourself.

# Tell him

When you tuck your toddler into bed, spend time giving him a cuddle and telling him what you've loved about spending time with him today. As you cast your mind back over the day's activities, congratulate yourself on finding ways that have made the day full and fun, but not pressured or frantic. As you paint a picture of the day again for him, you'll be giving him lovely thoughts as he drifts off to sleep, which will turn into memories of great days spent having fun with mum or dad.

# Condensed idea
## Frantic parents have frantic toddlers; fun parents have fun toddlers

## 32 Have a go!

Your toddler has no inbuilt idea of who she is or what she is capable of – she will learn that from you. As a parent, you can give her the courage to have a go and the belief that the world awaits – so she'll embrace challenges as exciting learning opportunities.

### Small steps to confidence

Your toddler will always want to do more and more. She's growing up in an exciting world that's full of possibilities and most toddlers are naturally inclined to 'have a go'. They are motivated to embrace new experiences and acquire new skills, but they will continually check back with their parents to see if their plans seem to have the seal of approval. A parent's part in the process is key, because a mum's or dad's signal that a task is safe is what gives a toddler the confidence to try new challenges and pick herself up again if she can't do it the first time.

If you push a toddler too hard to do something she's not ready to do, she'll dig her feet in and refuse to budge. If you are at her side, however, helping her to take small steps towards a realistic goal, she'll have the confidence to conquer them. Most importantly, you are there to help her handle her frustration and disappointment when she takes a step that is a bit too big and she can't quite make it.

### Praise effort, not just success

Your child is born without a sense of self: she has no real sense of who she is and what she is capable of achieving. But you act as her mirror. It is through looking at you and what you do and say to her that she learns

# Nurturing a 'have a go' toddler

You can help promote healthy self-esteem and encourage your toddler's natural enthusiasm to take on challenges in lots of different ways:

- Always give your toddler a few minutes to try to work something out for herself, rather than jump in and do it for her.
- When your toddler can't work out how to build a tower or do a jigsaw, give her a hand. Watch out for the warning signs and intervene before she gets too frustrated and gives up. If she is struggling, say, 'What can we try? Shall we try this way or that way first?' Give her a choice and let her decide. If it works, that's good. If not, she learns there is always another way to try.
- Encourage her to play with other children, as this will help her to learn to cooperate, negotiate and compromise.
- Praise her for handling difficult situations well. Say, for example, 'I can see you were unhappy with Mary when she wouldn't let you use the yellow paint you wanted, but it was good you carried on sharing yours with her.' You are acknowledging her feelings and praising the way she has behaved. This will make her want to do it again.
- Teach your child to problem-solve by sending her on a treasure hunt. Hide the treasure and give her simple clues to solve so that she can track it down.
- Make a point of asking her open-ended questions, so that she learns there is often no 'right' or 'wrong' answer and that she can come up with ideas of her own. When reading her a story, for example, you might say to her, 'What do you like about this book?'

to develop her sense of self and self-esteem. Your toddler's self-esteem is the value she attaches to herself; it is her armour against the challenges of the world. If she feels good about herself, she'll grow up able to resolve conflict. She'll be positive, motivated and live her life to the full. She will have a 'can do' attitude and believe she can find a way to overcome obstacles. She'll be a child who looks for solutions to problems.

This is why it's important to be a 'can do' parent. Be optimistic and have a go yourself. Show her that you aren't good at everything and you struggle with some things too, but you still give them a shot. Your toddler may even be better than you on a bike or scooter, and if so – let her know. Praise her for achieving things and for having a go and trying hard, even if she doesn't pull it off this time. It's important for toddlers to learn that parents are proud of their efforts, whatever the outcome. If she struggles to do up her shoelaces, for instance, instead of saying, 'Don't worry, you'll be able to do it soon,' say: 'I'm really proud of you for trying so hard.'

> I made myself stand back as Sofia went up the slide. Guess which of us was nervous? #standbydad

## Avoid labels

Your words are very powerful, so choose them with care. A few badly chosen or badly timed words may result in your toddler feeling incapable of doing something – or anything – correctly, resulting in her avoiding new experiences and activities. If you think she won't be able to do something, she will take this on board and think that there is no point in trying. Don't 'sum up' your child to other people in negative ways. For example, if she overhears a parent say something like: 'She's a bit slow at picking this up' or 'She's not very good at swimming' or 'She doesn't mix very well,' she'll take this as the truth, and the parent's words will become a self-fulfilling prophecy. Children trust their parents and take what they say at face value, so if mum or dad limits her potential, she will too.

# A bit of healthy competition

Every parent will have their own view on whether or not competition is healthy for children. I believe that healthy competition is good. If your toddler doesn't learn to lose, she never learns to win. Competition will encourage your toddler to take risks and rise to a challenge. It will help her learn about her strengths and weaknesses, and it's by learning to live with those little knocks that she'll learn to deal with bigger challenges later in life. It's important that children realize from the outset that life isn't fair and that sometimes, in some situations, they will lose or things won't go their way. If she learns that this is a fact of life now, it will help her to avoid disappointment and disillusionment later on when she becomes an adult.

## Condensed idea
### 'Can do' parents have 'can do' children

# (33) Team toddler

Your toddler has a very clear view of the world: he's the centre of the universe and you are there to do everything he wants. However, this will change over time as he learns about being part of a family team. There are lots of practical ways you can help.

## Other people count too

Your toddler firmly believes that the whole of life revolves around him and what he wants to do. You and others exist to do everything he wants and give him everything he needs. This means that he will only begin to take other people's feelings and needs into consideration if he is taught how to go about it. Parents have the exciting responsibility of helping toddlers to begin to understand that they are part of an amazing team – a family – and that even a toddler has lots to contribute in many different ways. As he grows up, your child will gradually learn that he is there for all of the family, just as they are there for him.

Parents can help to broaden their toddler's perspective and encourage him to think more about others by pointing out the positive impact of his good behaviour, by saying things like: 'I feel so proud of you for playing so well with Joe.' Whenever possible, give your toddler specific praise when he exhibits care for other people and their feelings, such as: 'It was kind of you to share your biscuit with Mary – you made her happy.' Always encourage him to talk about his own feelings and the feelings of other people. Gradually, he will learn the art of empathy and will begin to understand that what he does and says affects the way other people behave and feel. This is essential if family life is going to run smoothly.

# The family shape

When one of your children is a toddler, take a close look at your family team and make sure it is in good enough shape for your toddler to join. Lots of families come in the shape of an upside-down pyramid, with one person (often mum) at the bottom holding everyone up. That person can keep balancing everything for a while, but an upside-down pyramid

## Toddler team-building tips

There are lots of practical ways that are easy to put into practice in daily family life to help your toddler learn the value of teamwork:

- Use the word 'we' more often than 'I'.
- Whenever you see evidence of your toddler acting as a good sibling, acknowledge it out loud, by saying something like: 'You are a great brother. You can always make your sister laugh when she is upset. She really loves you.'
- Let your toddler help you with jobs. You can both have fun putting away toys, sorting clean washing, putting paper and boxes into the recycling bin, watering the garden – and lots more. Be realistic and break down the job into small steps for toddlers and bigger steps for bigger kids.
- Play family games together so that your toddler learns to take turns, share and play well with others.
- Establish fair family rules, for example, taking it in turns to choose what game to play, book to read or DVD to watch. Be consistent and he will learn about negotiation and compromise.

is not a very stable shape; if you take away the person acting as that bottom point, the shape collapses. This kind of family arrangement is unstable in the long run. In a strong team, every member has different strengths and responsibilities and all play a unique role that helps the family as a whole. A strong family is like a circle, where everyone has their feet on the ground, holds hands and supports one another. So think about what shape you want for your family team – the circle or the pyramid? Is your toddler going to learn to be a key member of the family circle – or be dependent on you and balance precariously on your shoulders?

The very best way to help your toddler learn to be an active member of the family team is to make sure that you are a great team player yourself. Mums often do things themselves rather than getting others to play their part. It's easy to understand why – because it's usually much quicker and easier. But good team leaders delegate and everyone – including your toddler – can make a valuable contribution to family life.

# Choosing to be a circle

Spending time together as a family is a great way to create a family circle. Everyday activities, such as eating all together, are important and can become an event where everyone gets involved. For example, the whole family can join in setting the table for a meal and clearing away. You may not be able to do it every day but do it at least once a week. Spending time with your extended family is also a great way to let your toddler see you being a great son or daughter or sister or brother yourself. Making time for your family in these ways will create memories that are priceless and that will last forever.

Creating a visual family tree will act as a constant reminder of what being a family is all about. Let your toddler help you collate photos of you all having fun as a family and add any pictures he draws too. Talk about what each member of the family does well and what you love about them.

> There is no 'I' in TEAM! If only my toddler could spell already... #teamleader

# Build your own traditions

Your family is unique and will have its own way of doing everyday things and celebrating special occasions. Toddlers love these. They are very important to his sense of belonging and when he grows up he will probably teach them to his own children. So whether it's family swimming on Saturday, Sunday lunch, or putting a pillow case at the bottom of his bed for Santa to fill with presents – create those family traditions.

## Condensed idea
### Build strong family bonds now and they will last a lifetime

# (34) Being social

There are certain things you'll probably never be able to do – like get your toddler to refrain from chatting while she's chewing. But there are lots of things you can teach her, such as how to behave with other people in a way that will help her make lots of friends.

## Do as I say, not as I do

You may not have realized, but your toddler has been learning about manners for ages. She's been keeping a close eye on you, learning everything you do. So if you want your toddler to have great manners, the easiest way to do it is to make sure that you have great manners too.

A toddler will say 'Please' and 'Thank you' if her parents do. That may sound obvious and you may be thinking that of course you do this, but try tuning into what you actually say to members of your family. You may find – like many people – that when it comes to your nearest and dearest, you begin to take what they do for granted without actually talking to them. You want your toddler to be polite, but do you always say 'Please' and 'Thank you' when you ask for the breakfast cereal? Do you occasionally grab the TV remote and switch channels without asking? What about thank-you notes? You may insist that your toddler draws a picture to say thanks to granny for a birthday present, but how good are you at writing your own thank-you notes? You may tell your toddler

> Manners maketh the toddler. And I'm sure she'll learn some one day! #greatexpectations

off for climbing on granny's sofa, but do you occasionally put your feet up on the furniture when you're watching TV? If you do everything you want your toddler to do, there's a very good chance that she will do it eventually too. Never forget that we are the models from which our children copy and learn.

## In private, in public

The other golden rule is to make sure that everything you do at home is equally okay in public. Lots of us would admit that we are a bit more relaxed about manners in our own home than when we are out and about. But your toddler doesn't have a two-tier system – she sees life in black and white. She will do everything she sees you do and everything she is allowed to do at home when she is with her grandparents, at the nursery, on a playdate or when you are visiting friends. She won't understand that other houses are different from her own house and so a whole new set of rules apply.

You may make your toddler laugh by putting a banana skin on your head at the meal table and pretending it's a hat, and she may love it when you turn a piece of kitchen roll into a plane and send it flying across the kitchen. You may laugh when your toddler passes wind – there's no right or wrong. But if you do that at home, don't be surprised when your little one does the same things when she's out in public.

# Top tips for politeness

There are many things you can do to help your toddler learn to be polite and courteous. Expect inconsistency, but keep at it. The important message is that people are polite and show respect because it's the right thing to do, not because manners are 'the rules':

- Remember to say 'Please' and 'Thank you' to children and adults – say, 'Thanks for coming' when her friend leaves after a playdate.
- Explain to your toddler the reason for politeness by saying something like: 'It is important to say "Please" and "Thank You" to show we appreciate other people helping us.'
- Encourage your toddler to say 'Hello' and 'Goodbye'. You can prepare her for this by saying: 'When we get to Sarah's house to play we're going to say "Hello" to Sarah and her mum.'
- Give specific praise when your toddler does something that shows awareness of someone else and their feelings, such as: 'You made grandma happy when you moved that chair for her.'
- Encourage your toddler to listen rather than interrupting. For instance: 'It is John's turn to talk. Listen to him, then when he has finished, you can talk'. Praise her for listening well.

# Teaching table manners

The family meal table is the perfect classroom for teaching manners. It takes time and energy, but little by little, you will see a difference. It's the best place to give her plenty of practice and start getting into good habits so that when you are out for Sunday lunch with friends or at the cinema or a wedding and she's required to sit down for a length of time, she can give it her best shot.

Start when your toddler is young, show and tell her how to behave at the table, and have realistic expectations. It's a big ask for her, because just sitting on a chair for more than a few minutes at a time is tough for a small child with a wriggling bottom. Toddlers are constantly on the move, so if you want her to learn to sit still, without rocking on her chair, get her to try it for a few minutes to begin with and then gradually build up the time. You can use an egg-timer to help her and make it more fun. Give your toddler very specific direction and set a good example. If you feel like you're not getting anywhere, and your toddler seems to be forever jumping off her chair, make sure you are not spending mealtimes constantly jumping up to load the dishwasher or answer the phone.

# Praise good manners

Draw attention to your toddler's good manners by praising her, rather than drawing attention to bad manners. In fact, ignore those as much as you can, because toddlers will repeat any behaviour that gets attention. Praise as often as you can, and make sure the whole family displays good manners. A toddler who learns to be polite when she is young has every chance of growing into a polite teenager.

# Condensed idea
## Your child was not born polite – she'll need to learn this from you

# (35) Staying connected

**Finding different ways to connect with your toddler is an important part of being a mum or dad. The stronger your connection, the happier you will both be in all aspects of family life. Play is not a luxury when it comes to your relationship with your toddler. It is vital.**

## Switch off the outside world

A survey of over 500 parents by the UK's Parent Coaching Academy reveals that 9 out of 10 mums and dads say they feel they have the strongest connection with their child when they are messing around, having fun together. They also say that this helps them to relax and forget about the stresses of family life. However, although many parents enjoy spending this important time with their children, actually creating the time to have fun when there is so much going on in busy family lives can be a real challenge (see pages 124–27). But without exception all parents agree that when they can find the time, they love it.

## Strong family relationships

Connecting with your child will be one of your most important achievements and it's best to start as soon as you can. All good relationships need working at – they don't just happen – and parent-toddler relationships are no exception. The more you put in, the more you will get out. The stronger your connection, the happier you will feel about all other parts of family life too. You're in a lifelong relationship with your child and you're laying important foundations now for years to come. You are nurturing a positive relationship that will be rewarding in the good times and help you both through more challenging times.

# 10 easy ways to make a connection

You're the expert at connecting with your toddler, so you'll already be doing so in all sorts of ways, but here are a few more tips to try:

- Smile, laugh and have fun together.
- Cuddle and kiss your toddler.
- Hold his hand. The old saying goes: 'Hold his hand for a short while and his heart forever.'
- Enjoy sharing a story together. Bring the story to life by acting it out, using lots of different character voices.
- Cheer up your toddler when he is upset. Give him a cuddle – show him you are there for him.
- Be excited with your child. Toddlers get excited easily and will love it when he knows you are feeling genuinely excited too.
- Do something together as a team – housework (you vacuum, he polishes), cooking a meal, doing a jigsaw or playing a game.
- Listen to your child with your heart and eyes as well as your ears.
- Love your toddler unconditionally – even when he makes it tough.
- Draw a heart on a brightly coloured piece of paper and leave it on his pillow.

## Relationships further afield

As well as developing his relationship with you, you are also teaching your toddler about the importance of relationships and communication in a much broader sense. As he grows older you'll want him to have positive relationships – with himself, with a wide circle of different family and friends – and, later, work colleagues and the community.

# The power of play

Spending time playing around, chatting and just doing things with you is one of the most important ways your toddler learns and develops. It helps him to understand about relationships and to understand how people relate to each other. It helps him to experience very positive feelings. By including him in your daily activities, you are also helping his physical, emotional, social and language skills develop.

So begin to see every day as an opportunity to strengthen your connection with your toddler and his world, and actively make a difference in his life. There are lots of things that you can do – not just in allocated 'play' time, when you're actively focused on him – but in everyday family life. Everything from chasing each other around the room when you both have a duster, to splashing and blowing bubbles in the bath, to singing loudly while you lay the table for a meal – it all counts. Any moment can become one in which you suddenly feel closer. Use as many of your senses as you can and encourage your toddler to enjoy doing that too. The easiest way to increase that sense of connection with him is to get down to his level and see the world through his eyes. While you're down there, ask yourself, 'What does he love doing with me? What do I love doing with him? What do we do that always makes us laugh together?'

Talk as much as you can to your toddler when you are enjoying time together. He may not have all the language to say everything he wants to, but he will love to hear your voice, and by listening to you he will be learning more than you can imagine. While he won't necessarily be able to respond to you verbally, he'll make his feelings known in lots of different and creative ways. So keep on chatting and communicating with your toddler – it will pay dividends in good behaviour, and you will be making him an even happier and more contented little person.

**Mum and dad come out to play!**
#youngatheart

# Spend time not money

Real connection with your toddler comes through spending time with him – not money. It can be tempting to buy toys, sweets or magazines for him, but it would be better to save your money and invest time instead. Toddlers will soon forget about expensive toys, but 10 minutes with mum or dad is priceless. You are your toddler's ultimate toy and any activity that you do together will be top of his fun list.

At times, it may seem difficult to build in times every day for really connecting with your toddler, but remember that just 10 minutes a day will make a difference. It doesn't need to be a special activity – joking around while you fold sheets together can be a close, connected moment. And don't forget to tell your toddler what you love about spending time with him. A few simple words will make him feel important and secure.

## Condensed idea
Laughing together is the most powerful
way to connect with your toddler

# Bumps in the night

It's totally natural for your toddler to be frightened of things – it's a normal part of her emotional development. Whether she's anxious about the dark, hearing loud noises, passing a dog, or being flushed down the toilet, there are strategies you can use to help.

## New fears are normal

It may take you by surprise when your little one suddenly cowers behind you when a dog barks, clings to you when you flush the toilet or screams when you turn the light off. This behaviour may be utterly new, and it may seem strange that she is reacting so differently to something that has never bothered her before. However, this is perfectly normal and it shows that her development is on track: many 18-month-old babies develop a fear of animals, noises and medical professionals; at two years of age, fears broaden to include the dark, toilets and people dressed strangely (such as clowns). At around two and a half, a toddler's imagination begins to develop, and her fears might include imaginary creatures. So at this age, a little bit of fear about something new, unexpected or overwhelming is a sign of healthy development.

## Small person, large world

Your toddler is learning to be independent and cope with her ever-expanding environment. She's very small in a world that's very big – and that can feel scary. She's developing a vivid imagination with which she can conjure up imaginary monsters behind the sofa and turn your vacuum cleaner into an alien from outer space. By two and a half, a toddler finds it hard to know what is real and what is imaginary.

# Common fears and how to help

Here are some strategies for you to try if your child suffers from any of the most common toddler fears:

- **Medical appointments:** prepare your toddler for visits to the doctor by playing with a toy medicine kit or reading a book about a child's visit to the nurse. If she's going for a vaccination, explain to her that it will sting a little and tell her that once it's done, you're both going to have fun together.
- **Dogs:** they can be scary and some do snap. When you see a dog, be practical and positive. Say to her: 'You can hold my hand and we will both walk past the dog together' or 'We can stand here and wait for the dog to go past us.' Let your toddler choose.
- **The dark:** your toddler's imagination will run wild in the dark. At bedtime, try using a nightlight and sit with her for a few minutes while her eyes adjust.
- **Monsters, witches or ghosts:** avoid reading stories with monsters too close to bedtime and don't watch DVDs that may fire her imagination. Reassure her by searching her room to make sure it is a monster-free zone.

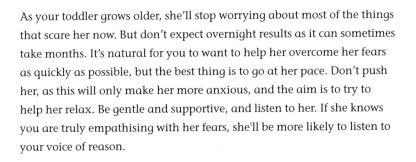

As your toddler grows older, she'll stop worrying about most of the things that scare her now. But don't expect overnight results as it can sometimes take months. It's natural for you to want to help her overcome her fears as quickly as possible, but the best thing is to go at her pace. Don't push her, as this will only make her more anxious, and the aim is to try to help her relax. Be gentle and supportive, and listen to her. If she knows you are truly empathising with her fears, she'll be more likely to listen to your voice of reason.

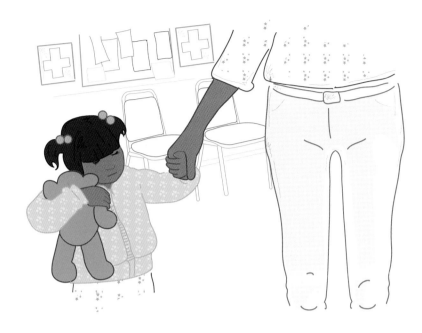

# Dealing with fears

If your toddler's worried about something, the most important thing to do is to give her a big cuddle. It's at times like this that she really needs to know that you are there for her. Always acknowledge her worries, so that she knows you are taking her feelings seriously. You may want to reassure her by saying, 'There's nothing to worry about because I won't let the dog hurt you' but it's better to let her know that you understand, by saying: 'I can understand why you are frightened of that dog, he's got a very loud bark.' It's important for your toddler to learn that it is okay to be afraid and that it's a good idea to let you know whenever this happens.

When talking about a particular fear, explain what is happening so that your child understands there is a reason for the thing that scares her. If, for example, she's anxious about loud noises like sirens, explain to her that a fire engine has to make a loud noise because it is in a hurry to help people and that when it uses its siren, it's letting cars know that it needs to pass them. If she's afraid of the plughole, tell her that water goes down there to empty the bath, but only liquids go down there.

Demonstrate with one of her bath toys and reassure her that toddlers are even bigger and definitely won't disappear down there.

If you know your toddler worries about something that's going to occur – such as being separated from you for a while – make sure you prepare her. If you are going to leave her with a friend, for example, let her know that it is going to happen and reassure her that you will return. Don't be tempted to sneak out without saying goodbye because then she'll never know when you are going to disappear. Lots of toddlers respond well to having a teddy or blanket that they can cuddle if they are worried. Give your child a choice of a couple of things – and let her decide what she wants to use to help comfort herself.

# Are you scared too?

It may be tough, but do everything you can to make sure you don't pass on your own fears and anxieties. If your toddler knows you are worried about something, the chances are she will be too. We can understand how our toddlers feel, because we all worry about things too, whether it's our health, our children, finances, parking the car – or spiders. It's good, however, to let her know that you were frightened of something as a child, perhaps visiting the dentist – and that you overcame it and now are happy to go to the dentist because he keeps your teeth healthy.

# Condensed idea
## Being a toddler can be scary, but you can do lots to reassure her

# (37) Early learning

**Toddlers are like sponges – they are always ready to soak up new information, experiences and knowledge. As a parent, there are lots of practical ways you can support what your child is learning and nurture his emotional, social and cognitive development.**

## Home is the best school

As your toddler develops, you will see all sorts of exciting changes in him. His confidence is growing, he's fascinated with life and he's into everything. He wants to find out all he can about himself and the world he is growing up in. It's natural for you to want to do all you can to help him on his journey, and that's great, because you will always be your toddler's best teacher. Also, you may be surprised to learn that your home is full of tools to teach your toddler lots of interesting things, so it isn't necessary to buy lots of expensive 'educational toys'.

However, don't get carried away! It's easy to fall into the trap of wanting to give your toddler the best possible start at school by starting his lessons early and putting a lot of emphasis on things like recognizing letters and numbers. Many parents do this and it's easy to understand why, especially when they are surrounded by other mums and dads constantly comparing all the children and their achievements. If someone asks if your toddler can count to 10 in a dozen different languages or say his alphabet backwards yet, don't take the bait. Smile, say 'No' and change the subject. You will always come across those who love nothing more than to boast about what a prodigy their child is. Ignore this competitiveness and try hard not to compare children yourself, because it can put you and your toddler under unnecessary pressure.

# Fun + engagement = learning

The very best way for children to learn is through engaging with them and making their learning an enjoyable part of what they are doing. As you will know from your own experiences, once any aspect of learning becomes a chore, toddlers – like all children (and especially teenagers) – will lose interest.

It is essential to remember that your toddler is at a very precious stage. Big, exciting school is just around the corner and it won't be long before he's there, with years of classroom learning in front of him. The very best way to help all aspects of his development is to help him enjoy himself now and feel comfortable in a wide range of environments and experiences. There are lots of great games and activities with educational elements that you can both have fun with – but do it in a very low key way. If you want to help him achieve his potential, make sure you don't put pressure on him to perform. Pressure will tempt a child (or anyone!) to put on the brakes. Fun, on the other hand, encourages engagement.

# Nurture your toddler's development

Here are some very practical ideas for helping your child's development while also having fun:

- Do things that your toddler naturally enjoys doing – whether this is visiting a playground or playing pick-up-sticks.
- Make sure you spend time talking with him about subjects he likes. This will help him build his vocabulary, especially if you make an effort to use lots of different words.
- Give him lots of opportunities to mix with other children and adults, and praise him for taking turns and sharing.
- Give him lots of practice at getting himself dressed and putting shoes and socks on.
- Help him to recognize his own name. Draw it together, use magnetic letters on a tray and make a sign for his bedroom.
- Nurture his natural desire to explore. Take him on an adventure into your garden or to the park and let him get up close to insects, fish and frogs.
- Introduce him to numbers in fun ways, such as by singing songs or reading books.
- Stimulate his love for songs and music with a variety of sounds to listen to and make.

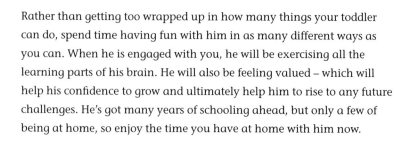

Rather than getting too wrapped up in how many things your toddler can do, spend time having fun with him in as many different ways as you can. When he is engaged with you, he will be exercising all the learning parts of his brain. He will also be feeling valued – which will help his confidence to grow and ultimately help him to rise to any future challenges. He's got many years of schooling ahead, but only a few of being at home, so enjoy the time you have at home with him now.

# Make books a priority

Reading to and with your toddler is probably the single most important thing you can do to help your child's education and it is likely to enrich his life now and throughout adulthood. When you are sharing books, relax and enjoy the stories together, letting your toddler get involved in the story by talking to him about the characters and the pictures. Don't be tempted to spend every story teaching him to read; he'll have plenty of time for that later. Create lots of different story opportunities – on the bus, in the bath and, of course, at bedtime. If you do only one thing towards deliberately encouraging your toddler's development, this is the one to focus on.

# Creativity needs to be messy

Toddlers love getting their hands dirty and take to all kinds of different art activities with relish. Arts and crafts are also great learning activities – getting his fingers around a chubby crayon, grappling with a paintbrush and experimenting with colour and materials will expand his imagination and develop his motor skills. Homemade birthday cards and pictures are always much better than those bought from the shop, and family members love them. Keep a few too – stick them up around your home and let him enjoy having his own art gallery.

> My toddler has been dreaming of going to the moon, just like the bear in his book. He's starry-eyed (and gorgeous). #bookmum

# Condensed idea
## The best way to nurture your toddler's development is to have fun together

# 38 Toddlercise

If you give your toddler a good dose of physical exercise, she's likely to be happy and healthy – and sleep well at nights too. Toddlers who are generally active and get regular exercise are likely to be better behaved and able to concentrate more effectively.

## How much exercise?

The UK National Association for Sports and Physical Education (NASPE) guidelines recommend that toddlers have at least 30 minutes of structured exercise (such as an adult-led swim, scooter ride or game of ball) and at least 60 minutes of unstructured activity (such as free play at the park or soft play) each day. Your toddler is growing and developing in lots of different ways and she's an absolute bundle of energy – you probably find yourself thinking that she's always ready for action. So introduce lots of exercise. As well as being good for her health, it's a good way to tire her out for bedtime too. The great thing is that exercise comes in lots of different forms. Your library or leisure centre is likely to have information about all sorts of local activity groups that your toddler can join if you want her to – but you don't necessarily have to join structured groups or paid exercise classes. The very best exercises are free.

## Crawl today, jump tomorrow

Toddler motor skills develop rapidly. It can seem as though they're crawling up the stairs one day, only to be jumping over puddles the next! Help your toddler to explore and experiment with what she can physically do. Whether she's crawling, beginning to toddle around or walking, find some fun things to keep her on the move that are tailored to her developmental stage. Keep fun a priority and encourage her to try things she's never done before, but don't put her under pressure to perform or move on to the next stage before she is ready.

# Get out and about

You and your toddler will benefit from a breath of fresh air at least once a day. She'll enjoy sunshine, wind or rain if you are positive about it, so don't let the weather put you off. Walking is one of the very best exercises and it's easy to do on a daily basis. If you can build walking into your daily life, you and your toddler will be active without really thinking about it and you'll have a great opportunity to chat together. Also, if she gets used to walking now, she won't expect to be driven everywhere as she gets older. So start building walking into your daily life and do it whenever you can instead of driving or taking the bus, whether it's to the supermarket, park or library. If you generally use a pushchair, make sure she gets out to walk for at least some of the way. Walk as though you love it – if she sees you are enjoying it, she will too.

# Encouraged by others

Your toddler's interest in sport and physical activity is really just beginning. If she learns to love these things now, she's more likely to want to do them when she is older. Siblings and older children can be great motivators for toddlers. If a toddler sees an older brother, sister or cousin enjoying street dance, football, swimming or cycling, she'll want to have a piece of the action too. If she knows that you like standing on the touchline watching, or being in the audience at a ballet show, she'll be only too keen to join in when she's old enough.

> No need for a personal trainer – my toddler seems to be giving me a pretty effective workout!
> #runningmum

Another way to encourage your toddler to be active is by giving her an audience – all children love to be the centre of attention. Put some music on and encourage her to dance – tell her that she is the star of the show and you are her biggest fan, or put your dancing shoes on and join in!

# Toddler trainer

The good news about all of this is that there is no need for you to sign up for a year's membership at the local gym to get fit, because you can work out with your very own personal trainer – your toddler. Your child can increase your levels of fitness, health, vitality and zest for life. She'll be the best personal trainer you could hope for and she's there 24/7. She has endless energy and lots of get-up-and-go, so follow her lead. A toddler can keep you incredibly fit if you want her to, and you can both have fun at the same time. Exercise that you enjoy will be exercise that you are motivated to do and are likely to make part of your daily routine. Your toddler also provides your biggest motivation to stay fit and healthy, because you'll want to be around for as long as possible for her – and to have enough energy to be the mum or dad you want to be.

# Fun ways to toddlercise

Although you're probably both already running around all day, purposeful exercise doubles up as a fun game that you can play together. Here are a few more ideas for you to try:

- Play physical games such as 'Follow my leader'.
- Dance together. Put on a couple of songs you both love and get out there and enjoy yourselves.
- Doing jobs is a great way to incorporate exercise – laying the table, watering the garden and cleaning the car.
- Choose toys and games that promote activity, such as running after a ball or chasing bubbles.
- Set up an obstacle course in your living room and have fun racing over and under cushions and pillows.
- Take your toddler along to your local soft play area. Go with a friend who has a toddler for double the fun.
- Go swimming together. Find out about float sessions at your local pool and the whole family can have fun.
- Build fun activities into holidays and family days out – enjoy walking, hiking, cycling and swimming.
- Run down a hill in the spring, paddle in the summer, walk through leaves in autumn and jump over puddles in winter.

## Condensed idea
### Daily physical exercise is fun and great for your toddler's health and wellbeing

**Making sure that your toddler is eating a healthy, balanced diet with regular, nutritious snacks is essential if you want to avoid toddler tantrums – if he is hungry, he will soon go into meltdown. A toddler may also use food as a weapon to get his own way, so beware.**

## The link between food and behaviour

We took a look at strategies to avoid food fights earlier (see pages 28–31) because parents can find mealtimes extremely stressful. This chapter highlights the connection between food and tantrums and gives you an insight into why a toddler acts as he does around food. There are two

important sides to this situation: his and yours. He will know instinctively that any situation involving food has the potential to give him the upper hand, if you let him. At the same time, it's easy to blame your toddler for his 'fussiness' when more often than not, he's reacting to the way you feed him. Luckily, there are some practical tools you can use to make a positive difference to your toddler's behaviour around food, whatever the situation. Essentially, by making changes to your attitude towards his eating habits, you can change his attitude too.

# Sweet treats

Research shows that in lots of cases, parents may be to blame for the challenging way their toddler behaves. In a survey of 300 mums and dads (by the Parent Coaching Academy, UK, 2012), 8 out of 10 parents admit to 'bribing' their toddlers with unhealthy snacks to get them to do what they want. It's easy to understand why this happens, given the pressures of daily life, and most of us will admit to having been there. In fact, there are lots of reasons why we do it. Some of us use the promise of a 'sweet' or 'treat' to get a toddler to eat something that we want him to eat first. If he will eat his carrots, we might say we'll give him a sticky pudding. Sometimes the bribe works, and a packet of sweets at the supermarket checkout that stops our toddler screaming seems worth its weight

> Wouldn't it be easier to give in to screaming demands for 'chockie' than ignore them? #losingcontrol

in gold. On the other hand, many of us offer sweets because we were given 'sweet treats' when we were small by our parents, and we carry on the tradition. Many working parents say they do it because they've been away from their children all day and want to give them something they know they like.

You may only give your toddler sweet treats now and again. But the problem here is that your toddler gets a very clear message: 'If I behave in a certain way (eating my vegetables, kicking off in the supermarket or making mum or dad feel guilty for being at work all day), they will behave in a certain way and give me whatever I want to eat.' Whenever you stick to your guns and refuse to offer a bribe, your toddler will be confused as to why this time is different to the last time, when he got his own way. Being consistent is the key to a well-behaved toddler. Sweet treats can also turn your toddler into a fussy eater (and toddlers are notoriously picky in any case). He may end up eating broccoli only on condition that you give him pudding afterwards, rather than learning to eat it on its own.

# Make healthy snacks yummy!

If you do sometimes find yourself resorting to 'sweet' bribes, or offering them as treats or rewards, try one or two of these ideas to change what you do. You'll be pleasantly surprised by the change in your toddler's behaviour:

- Don't assume that your toddler prefers sweet treats to healthy snacks. Be patient if he refuses something you offer him, and try it again another day. He may reject carrot sticks today but love them tomorrow.
- Set a great example. Find some really healthy snacks that you want to eat instead of reaching for the cake tin. They're as good for you as they are for him.
- You may not always be able to control what your toddler wants to eat, but you can control what you buy. Only buy food you want him to eat; leave the rest on the supermarket shelf.
- Put healthy snacks (that you can both eat) in bowls around the house to encourage healthy grazing.
- Tune in to what you say about food and choose your words carefully. Make sure you say, 'Delicious – I love carrots dipped in tzatziki!' instead of 'A chocolate digestive – what a treat!'
- Avoid saying to your toddler, 'If you eat this... I will do this...' If you give him an ultimatum, he's likely to say, 'No'.
- Praise your toddler for eating healthy food. Be specific. Instead of saying, 'Well done for eating that', say: 'Well done for eating that yummy red pepper. Was it nice and crunchy?'
- Keep your resolve by focusing on the many benefits healthy snacks have for your toddler – and for you.

Effective though it appears to be at first, bribing with sweets and treats doesn't work. In the long term, it will only make your toddler's behaviour worse. Take a positive and calm approach to tantrums – during and between meals – and focus on praising your toddler for behaving well and eating well. It's a much more effective approach.

## Hungry toddlers aren't happy

If your toddler is rested with a full tummy, his behaviour is likely to be much more positive and fun than if he's hungry. If he has no petrol in his tank, he is much more likely to be grouchy and behave in a more challenging way. Toddlers are always active – they are little adventurers exploring the world and their lifestyle lends itself to snacking and grazing, not sitting down to meals. So it's a good idea to have a range of healthy snacks available, such as toddler-sized slices of apple or banana; carrot, pepper and courgette sticks; mini tuna or cheese sandwiches; natural yogurt and fromage frais with chopped fruit or bread sticks for dipping. Healthy snacks like these provide the energy and nutrition that your toddler needs to make the most of his day.

## Worried about his eating?

Toddler eating habits can be very unpredictable – with tastes changing frequently or staying fixed on just a few items for weeks at a time. Don't worry if his diet seems repetitive occasionally; it's fine as long as it's nutritionally adequate. You might think that there's a reason he will only eat peanut butter sandwiches, but it's likely to be just a passing phase. If you are at all concerned about what your toddler is or isn't eating, or have any concerns about allergies, always talk to your doctor.

## Condensed idea
### Your attitude to what your toddler eats will affect his behaviour

# 40  Parenting milestones

Every day, you'll see your toddler change slightly, as she accomplishes exciting major milestones such as walking and talking. There are, however, other more challenging milestones you might feel less excited about, but which are just as vital to her development.

## Personal challenges

You may have been charting your toddler's development with pride, marking up a height chart in the hall or noting down first words in a special book. (Don't worry if you've been meaning to do that but haven't had time to get around to it – most parents don't. It's a great idea in theory but often difficult in practice, given the pace of family life.) However you notice or mark milestones, every parent feels proud when their toddler reaches them, whether this is a sudden interest in trying new types of food or occasionally sitting on the potty.

Some milestones, however, on the route to independence might provoke a different response in you. When your toddler begins to disagree with you, your instinctive response might be that she's being cheeky. When she insists on doing everything for herself, you might feel a twinge of regret that she's growing up, or infuriation that she's taking so long to do something. But these early manifestations of independence are important 'growing up' milestones, in just the same way as using a

> Ella was very cheeky today. I kind of admired her while also feeling really annoyed! #powerstruggle

potty or finding new words. They mean that your toddler is developing in absolutely the right way, so it's important to recognize and celebrate these too. Once you understand the phases she is going through and the reasons why, you'll be able to handle her challenging behaviour in a much more positive way.

## Limiting choices

When your toddler starts to make her own decisions, it's a sign of healthy social and emotional development. It's a great world out there full of possibilities, but she's only recently become aware that this means there are lots of choices to be made: she can choose what to wear, what to eat, and how to spend her time. If she wants to wear a T-shirt in the middle of winter or eat a plate of biscuits instead of broccoli – why shouldn't she? You'll need to balance her need to flex these 'choosing' muscles against your need to keep the day roughly on track and her food reasonably healthy. So let her exercise her ability to choose, but limit the choices to a couple of areas that you feel happy with.

This new stage may challenge you for several reasons. It can be totally exasperating waiting for a child to reach a decision – often extremely slowly – when you're under pressure and need to go somewhere. Your toddler may begin to see choices everywhere, and either talk them all through thoroughly, or refuse to talk them through at all. However your toddler starts to exercise choice, remember that the fact that she's determined to make her own decisions shows that she's becoming confident. She wants to be in the driving seat in her own life, and that's a good goal for her to aim for.

# Change your own thinking

If you notice that you're feeling challenged by your toddler's behaviour, take a deep breath and remind yourself about what's really happening – your toddler is showing signs of healthy development. Here are some ideas to help you:

- When your toddler begins to show signs of defiance, say to yourself: 'I can handle this. This is supposed to happen. It's a sign she's learning to be independent and that's a good thing even if it feels annoying right now.'
- When she refuses to take directions, say to yourself: 'She's showing she's excited about the world. She wants to explore it and tell me about it, but isn't able to communicate in a way I can understand. I need to listen more carefully.'
- When your toddler does something that you specifically told her not to do, say to yourself: 'She's showing just how curious she is. It's human nature to want to touch, drink, eat and smell the things you are banned from. And she's testing boundaries, so I need to stay calm while reminding her of them.'

# Bye bye baby, hello toddler!

As toddlers become more independent, you might suddenly find yourself feeling that you've become surplus to requirements. It seems that suddenly she's decided that she wants to do everything herself, even if she can't really do it. It can be shocking to realize that gone are the days when you did everything for her – she's set now on doing everything herself. She wants to feed herself, brush her hair, pour her own drinks, dress herself – even if this means she sometimes ends up wearing her pants on her head. And when you explain the right and wrong ways to do it, she probably won't be interested. She knows exactly how she wants it to be done and that's the way she's going to do it.

It's an important milestone, and it's being played out right in front of you. Don't interfere (unless she's in danger) or you will stop her from reaching it. Your little one is taking a big step, from being fully dependent on you to becoming independent. Notice how this makes you feel, because if you're struggling to accept that your baby has grown into an independently minded child, your temptation will be to step in and help all the time, delaying her development. Instead, congratulate her progress and your own great parenting, which has led to this strong sense of self.

Let your toddler really enjoy her first taste of independence as much as you can. Instead of thinking, 'I can't believe what a mess she's made,' think, 'This is my little girl learning to do things for herself – I love her for that.' It may seem a long way off, but one day (hopefully!) she'll be making your breakfast and setting up your new mobile phone. So sit back and enjoy watching her practise her fantastic, new-found skills.

## Condensed idea
### Celebrate your toddler's steps towards independence even when you find them tough to handle

# (41) Managing your time

Many parents find themselves thinking, 'There just isn't enough time to do everything!' It can sometimes feel as though you'll never fit everything in, no matter how hard you try. But small changes to daily planning can make a big difference and free up time for fun.

## Be positive about time

Whenever you worry that, as a parent, you don't have enough time, that very thought puts you under pressure. The key to feeling that you do have enough time lies with you, because it's about your frame of mind. It's also worth noticing that worrying about lack of time makes you feel more worried, not less. So instead of wasting time on worrying, invest your time in doing something positive. Value your time as a gift, rather than devaluing it as a burden. Instead of thinking, 'What will I do? There are only 24 hours in the day and I'll never fit everything in!' start saying: 'Great – I've got a whole 24 hours – what shall I do with it?' In this way, instead of running after time, you'll be taking control of it from the start. Rather than talking about what you haven't done, start telling people what you have achieved with your time. Your toddler will quickly pick up on your new, positive attitude.

## Learn to say 'No'

Mums and dads tend to say 'Yes' to everything they are asked to do because they want to help. But saying 'Yes' when you really want to say 'No' means that you'll have less time to do what you want to do, putting yourself under greater pressure. When we become parents, our lives become a whole lot busier and it's easy to get caught up in the day-to-day

bustle without reflecting on what we're doing. This might be the perfect time to take a good look at your own life – including your hopes and wishes – and focus on moving that in the right direction, before trying to look after everyone else.

## Do, drop or delegate

Parents often try to do everything themselves because they think that it's easier and quicker than delegating to another member of the family team. Mums, in particular, can be guilty of this. Dads often say that they'd like to do more, but their partner knows exactly what she wants and insists on it being done that way, so the dads back away, ultimately leaving everything to mum. If you find yourself thinking that you're doing everything, try the 'do, drop or delegate' technique for a week; you'll be surprised at how much time this creates for yourself. Prioritize your activities and only do the ones that are vital or that you really want to do. Drop the ones that aren't a priority and delegate whatever you can to other members of the family (including grandparents). As well as creating time for you, delegating gives other people the opportunity to take responsibility and feel involved.

# How important is the housework?

Many parents say that one of the main reasons they get stressed and don't have enough time with their toddlers is because of all the jobs around the house that need doing. But there is another way to look at it: there will always be something that needs doing and if you're not careful, instead of controlling the housework, you'll find the housework controlling you. Some women have spent years trying to create the perfect family home before realizing that it doesn't exist. Family homes have families in them – they are lived in, so they show the messy signs of life. The fact that your home may often resemble a crime scene is part of your family adventure. If you find it hard to live with a little mess, imagine your house perfectly clean and tidy, because there's no one but you living there, isn't it preferable to have mess and people around you? Why not decide now to limit the time you spend on the housework so that you can spend more time with your child? When your toddler is grown up with children of his own, you can rest assured he won't be telling them how well you made the beds. He'll be telling them about the experiences you shared as a family and he'll remember the fun, lively home – not the tidy, vacuumed house.

> Help! 24 hrs not enough! Need some kind of superpower! #frazzledmum

# Go out and have fun!

Stop planning, stop thinking about all of the things you should really be doing, leave the housework – and the home – and just go out and have fun. It's the simplest way to create more time with your toddler. You will always find a way to do the stuff you left behind, or you may find, after a good run around the park, that whatever seemed so pressing is not so important after all. Slow down and treasure every moment. Don't go to bed thinking about what you haven't done today – drift off thinking about what you have enjoyed today in your role as mum or dad.

# Top tips for creating more time

Children grow up amazingly fast, so don't let that time slip away. Here are some ideas for creating more time with your family:

- Make life easy for yourself. Put some ready-made meals in the freezer for those days when you're short on time.
- Use the 'quick wash' setting on the washing machine and don't iron anything unless it can't be worn without being pressed.
- Limit the time you spend on housework. Instead of saying 'I'll do it until I finish,' say: 'I'm giving myself 30 minutes to do as much as I can.' You'll be much more productive.
- Leave work on time: put your family first.
- Set boundaries for your mobile (calls, texts and emails) so that you are not on call 24/7. Reserve special family time by switching off your phone when you go out.
- If you work from home, shut your office door when you want to leave work and switch off your computer.
- Cut down on your toddler's social life. Decide how many playdates or clubs you want your toddler to go to and stick to it.
- Set up a support network with other parents and give each other time off, or ask the grandparents to babysit on a regular basis.
- Buy shopping and presents online.

## condensed idea
**Life is about choices and you can create more time if you want to**

# 42 Creating 'me' time

As any parent will tell you, it's impossible to imagine just how much energy it takes to look after a toddler, let alone find time for anyone else. But as parents, you're a team – you need to nurture yourself and your relationship to be the best mum or dad you can be.

## Take time for yourself

Most parents are rushing around all day, every day. They are always on the go – at home and at work – and may not sit down from the moment they get up until the time they go to bed. Relaxing and putting themselves first isn't something that comes naturally to parents.

However, if you want to be a good parent, it's essential to put yourself first sometimes. You need to be on top form for your toddler and have enough energy to match hers, which means you need to look after yourself and recharge your batteries occasionally. By creating 'me' time, you'll boost your energy levels and cut your stress levels. You'll live longer, feel happier and rise to the challenges of family life more easily if you are not exhausted. Most importantly, you'll have lots more fun with your toddler and this will have a positive impact on the whole family. 'Me time' isn't selfish – it's a must!

A 2012 survey of 500 parents by the UK's Parent Coaching Academy found that dads find it easier to enjoy 'me' time than mums. Mums say they find it harder to 'switch off' when there is so much to do, whereas dads say that taking time out is a priority for them – and they're most likely to choose to spend it with friends, at the gym or watching sport. Mums consider any time without toddler in tow as 'me' time, even if this means doing the shopping or housework. However, being alone but still doing all the jobs that need doing doesn't count: for 'me' time to be effective, it has to be a real treat. It might be a long soak in the bath, a walk, a massage, or an hour playing sport or curled up on the sofa with a good book and no interruptions.

## Too tired to tango?

All good relationships need working at; they don't just happen. Having children can bring couples closer together, but it is also likely to bring some tough challenges which will call for a lot of patience, understanding and thoughtfulness from both sides. Being a parent of a toddler is tiring, and when you're both exhausted, it can be easy to take each other for granted and be negative with each other, which in turn can cause a build-up of resentment. There's always so much to do and think about that even finding time to talk to each other is difficult. And when you do, you probably find you are talking about facts – such as who is going to do the weekly shop, cook dinner or change the nappy this time – instead of talking about your feelings for each other. But if there's one thing that is vital in a relationship, it's communication.

Surveys have revealed that while dads see making love as a priority, it's often at the bottom of a mum's 'to do' list, mainly because she is just too tired. Dads can sometimes take this lack of enthusiasm personally and feel resentful of this change in the relationship. Finding time to talk to each other about your feelings can help avoid a wall building between you. After all, keeping your relationship strong in all areas will be beneficial, not only for you and your partner, but also for your children: a solid family structure means a happier home environment. So make it a priority to spend time talking together and try not to put pressure on

# Happier families

You are a team and together you are stronger. It's essential that you nurture your relationship with each other to build a happy home for your toddler: well-behaved toddlers are happy toddlers. Here are some ideas for you to try with your partner:

- Book a babysitter and take your partner out on a 'date'. Treat it as a toddler-free zone – don't talk about your children.
- Pack a special picnic. Go somewhere peaceful and beautiful away from the crowds for a few hours.
- Spend a romantic night together – at home, in a tent or at a hotel. Enjoy the opportunity to sleep late in the morning.
- Reminisce together. Get out your pre-children holiday photos or watch the first film you ever saw together.
- Tell your partner often that you love them. Focus on what you love about them – and let them know. Say it, text it, email it or put a sticky note on the bathroom mirror.
- Learn something new together, such as salsa dancing, sailing or a foreign language.

one another. Whilst maintaining a good sex life is important for a lot of couples, kissing and cuddling and generally showing that you care for one another is just as important too.

## Making it happen

The important part is to make 'me' time and 'us' time happen and the best way to do this is to put it in your diary. If you say you are going to go for a swim at 2 p.m. on Saturday, it is much more likely to happen than if you say you are going to squeeze it in over the weekend. And making it a regular weekly event will give you something to look forward to.

If you are arranging 'me' time, talk to your partner and plan to give them 'me' time, too. If you are organizing 'us' time, book the grandparents or talk to friends and arrange a regular time when they can look after your toddler – you can return the favour for them on another day.

Try to find ways to build 'me' time and 'us' time into daily life too – for example, when your toddler is taking a nap. If you think it sounds decadent, just try it and see; you'll soon discover that if you take a break, you'll be much more productive than when you try to keep going all day. In the evenings when your toddler is in bed, switch your mobiles and computers off and regard your evenings together as precious. This is an ideal time to switch off from your roles as parents and enjoy one another.

> Out for dinner with partner for the first time in a year. What on earth will we talk about? #toddlerfreezone

## Condensed idea
### 'Me' time and 'us' time are vital for a happy, healthy family

# 43 De-stress yourself

The pressures of family life can seem overwhelming at times. But if you become stressed, your toddler will pick up on this and it may affect him physically or mentally. Developing a positive attitude to stress is important for you, your toddler and the whole family.

## Acknowledge stress

You may have noticed that since you became a parent, you seem to worry more. Many mums and dads say that as well as worrying about major issues such as health, finance and childcare, they also worry about smaller things such as organizing a babysitter or sorting out a packed lunch. There are lots of good reasons to learn to handle stress well; apart from the fact that you'll be happier and healthier, with lots more energy to enjoy your family, the way you rise to the challenges of family life will have an impact on the world your toddler grows up in. Research has shown that children appear to 'catch' their parents' stress, exhibiting behavioural problems or even illness in response to being with a very stressed parent. As a parent, you're also teaching your child how to tackle problems in his own life, so if you learn to handle stress well, he will too. It's important to acknowledge how you feel – in the same way that you encourage your toddler to talk about how he is feeling. Being honest about what is worrying you is the first step to handling stress.

## Do something

There are always certain factors outside your control, but if you want to reduce your stress levels there are two things you must do. First, think positive and believe you can make changes. The more you worry about feeling stressed, the more stressed you will become and in this state, you're not so much living as existing. If you feel under pressure and start to worry too much, your imagination can start to run wild. As a stay-at-home parent it's easy to feel as though you're doing everything alone, and this feeling of isolation can make it harder to think clearly.

## Quick ways to lower stress levels

There are lots of ways to reduce your stress levels if you want to. If you're feeling stuck, choose one of the following ideas and you'll soon notice a difference:

- Get fit and have fun with your toddler. Go for a run or swim together, or try out parent-and-toddler gym or yoga lessons.
- Take control of the household budget. Set a fixed amount for your weekly shop and stick to it.
- Talk to your partner about what is worrying you and work out what you can do together to make things better.
- Identify all of the people who can help make your life easier in a practical way, especially friends and family. Ask them to do one specific, practical thing to help you.
- Say 'I can' more often than 'I can't'.
- Take up yoga or learn to meditate.
- Enjoy a healthy diet. Always eat breakfast, drink plenty of water and eat healthy snacks including fruit and vegetables.
- Get fresh air every day, for at least 10 minutes.
- Surround yourself with positive people. Contact someone you really enjoy seeing, put it in your diary and make it happen.
- Enjoy being a 'real' mum or dad and don't put yourself under pressure to be a 'super' or 'perfect' parent.

Begin by spending a few minutes remembering what's going well in your life and what you have to be thankful for. It doesn't have to be perfect – nobody's life is perfect, so don't waste time wishing for this unattainable state. Second, decide to take action. If you're feeling stressed, you need to think and act differently; continuing with what you are already doing means nothing will change. Decide to take action, then take it, one step at a time, moving forward in a new direction. You can't control other people or what they do, but you can take responsibility

> Have decided it's time to stop worrying and start living. #wisemum

for yourself – for what you do and how you feel. The more you feel your life is out of control, the greater your stress levels will be. To reduce them, you need to take control and put yourself back in the driving seat.

## Strategic focusing

Don't try to tackle everything at once – focus on one specific area at a time and take action. Once you have control over that particular issue, you can move onto the next. For example, if you are stressed about your toddler crying when you leave him in someone else's care, set up a time to sit down and talk to the childminder, so you can develop a joint action plan. Then, if you are worried about money, make time to sit down and make a list of both the income you have and what you currently spend. Challenge yourself to, say, save £25 on your monthly outgoings, and you may be surprised to find that you can usually see a way to do it. Perhaps another issue that is making you feel stressed is that you are missing your child's bedtime every night. Take control by committing to leave work on time at least once a week so that you're back in time to put your toddler to bed.

Tackling your worries one step at a time is easier than taking on everything at once – which will seem overwhelming and impossible. And ultimately, taking action now will lead to a happier, less stressful life.

# De-clutter

De-cluttering is a very effective way to cut your stress levels and boost your energy levels. It needn't take long – if you challenge yourself to make a difference in 10 minutes, you'll probably succeed.

There are three obvious ways you can de-clutter and feel better, so consider doing one, two or all three of them. The easiest one to start with is to de-clutter your toddler's toy boxes, books, wardrobe and rucksack. Then move up a notch and de-clutter your home, or at least one part of it, such as your clothes, your desk, a kitchen cupboard. Or part of the car – maybe the boot. Lastly, and most effectively, de-clutter your mind of negative thoughts. They drain your energy, sap your spirit and generally make you feel less able to cope. Find somewhere quiet to sit, then close your eyes and silently count down from 30. As you count, take deep breaths and become aware of the breath moving in and out of your body. Imagine your breath as a wind, blowing out old negative thoughts. As your mind clears, fill the empty space with positive thoughts and a vibrant picture of you and your toddler laughing. This meditative technique can work wonders on stress and is a simple and practical exercise that you can practise anywhere and at any time.

## Condensed idea
### Your toddler learns how to handle pressure from watching how you handle it

# 44 Feel good, not guilty

Some days you'll really enjoy being a parent and feel great. On other days, though, things can feel really tough, and it's at this point that an irrational sense of guilt can kick in. This can be damaging for you and your toddler, so here are some ways to think differently.

## The negative power of guilt

Guilt is a strong emotive word. You usually hear it in the courts when people are accused of criminal activity, not in everyday life. However, many parents, especially mums, say they often feel guilty. What's more, they usually say it's a word they rarely used about themselves before they had children – perhaps occasionally if they had a third piece of cake. But as parents they find themselves using it on a regular basis. It is important to realize that this is potentially damaging; guilt can have

a profound effect on the way you feel about yourself as a parent and on family life. Be honest about how you feel, and if you feel guilty, stop and take a reality check. Are you really doing something that bad?

While all parents feel guilty at one time or another, parents who go out to work seem to have the biggest problem with it. They're really struggling to combine two very demanding roles – at home and at work – and can easily feel they are failing at both. Juggling family and work is a huge challenge, especially if you're doing it for the first time. Feeling guilty about being away from your toddler – and then being tired and a bit cranky with them when you are back at home together – is perfectly natural. Every

> Feeling bad about missing nursery concert, even though Fred's just banging a drum. #soredad

mum and dad knows what that's like, whether they work away from home or not. But staying stuck in guilty feelings will only make things worse, so identify what it is that makes you feel guilty and take action. Doing something that is within your control and relevant to whatever you're feeling bad about will help reduce those guilty feelings.

# Rechannel your thoughts

What is really going on is that you love your toddler and the reason why you're feeling stressed about leaving her is because you're passionate about being the best parent possible – and that's something to feel good about. So remind yourself that you are a good parent and that you're going to feel good when you're at home with her. The best way to ensure this is to look after yourself at work (guilt thrives in parents who are tired and feeling vulnerable). Boost your healthy eating habits and get some fresh air at lunchtime. Most importantly, don't let your imagination run riot by convincing yourself that your child is unhappy because you are not with her. You've chosen a good childcare option and you're leaving your toddler with someone you like and trust; so don't make

# Top 10 guilt-busting tips

The more you talk about feeling guilty, the worse you'll feel. So challenge yourself to get through the day feeling good instead of guilty. The key is to focus on the time you are with your toddler and make the most of that, rather than dwelling on the time you are away. Use some of the following tips to get you on track:

- Stop using the word 'guilty'. Talk to your toddler about what makes you feel good about being her mum or dad.
- Change out of your 'work' clothes when you get home and get into your 'parent' clothes and mindset.
- Make playdates with your toddler and do something fun each week. Put them in your diary and make them happen.
- Switch your mobile and computer off and put them out of sight. Schedule special time with your toddler without interruptions.
- Leave work at work (this takes time and commitment to crack) and be 100 per cent mum or dad when you are with your toddler.
- Don't make false promises. Say what you mean and mean what you say – and you won't feel guilty about breaking your word.
- Spoil your toddler with time, not money. Find 10 minutes to play with her instead of spending £10 on a toy for her.
- Make the most of bedtimes. You may not be able to be there every evening, but make the most of the times you can. Give your toddler a cuddle, share a book and tell her what you love about being with her.
- Make meal times with your toddler special. Have breakfast together if possible, or make meals at weekends a big family affair if you are not with the rest of the family during the week.

your journey to and from the nursery or childminder a guilt trip; make it fun. One guaranteed way to make you feel stressed is to think of the many things your toddler might be missing out on by being at nursery. Think instead about all the activities she is enjoying while she is there, all the benefits she gets from mixing with other adults and children, and how you might have been at home with her but would probably have been busy with the laundry or cleaning. Don't imagine her sitting alone being unhappy – picture her playing, surrounded by friends, and learning new things, because that's the real situation. Find some really good photos of your toddler laughing and surround yourself with them – on your desk, phone, mouse mat and jacket pocket. That way, you can remind yourself of how much fun your toddler is having and that it's you that's suffering, not her!

## Find out about making changes

You may be able to make changes in your working week that will make a difference. Rather than focusing on the problems, focus on the solutions to your working challenges and talk to your line manager about them. You may be able to reduce your hours (if you can afford to) or build in some flexibility (by starting work earlier and finishing earlier). You may even be able to organize working from home one or two days a week, which will cut out commuter time and enable you to spend those extra hours with your toddler.

Find out if your employer has a Parent Support Network or see if they are interested in setting one up. This is a really effective way for parents to support other mums and dads by sharing their experiences and ideas, and may help to provide a solution to the things you are worried about.

## Condensed idea
### Don't waste time feeling guilty – use it to create better strategies

# (45) Mind the gap

**It's normal for mums and dads to agree on some things about parenting and strongly disagree on others. Sometimes it's healthy to have different perspectives but at other times it's essential you come to a compromise so that you both send your toddler one clear message.**

## Learning from each other

Mums and dads often do things differently and by combining your approaches you can work as a team to get a real balance in family life. Lot of mums, for example, say they are 'helicopter' parents, hovering around their toddlers to make sure absolutely nothing can happen to them. Dads say they tend to take a 'black run' approach and are more willing to stand back and let the children take safe risks. Mums say they like to plan and check. Dads are more likely to act on the spur of the moment. Mums say they are the logistical experts and often it is dad who has the fun. Mum will empty the dishwasher because it needs doing. Dad's much more likely to leave it and take his toddler to the park instead. One parent is quicker to jump in (picking up a toddler when he falls off his scooter, for instance), while the other holds back (waiting for him to get back on his own). These are stereotypes, but it's surprising how often couples fall into different roles, and, in fact, all of these approaches are healthy in different ways. You will both have great ideas as parents, so learn from each other and use a bit of both.

> Arjun seems to know exactly which button to press to get dad to say yes! #playingthegame

# Clear messaging

There are times, however, when it is essential to ensure that mum and dad both send the same clear message to their toddler about key aspects of how they want him to behave. If the two of you can't agree about what time he's supposed to go to bed, how are you going to deal with his tantrums come bedtime? And if you can't agree on what constitutes table manners, what approach are you going to take when he fires Weetabix across the kitchen? The problem here is that if you say different things, your toddler will end up confused and won't know which is the right thing to do.

You and your partner may not agree on everything, but you have to negotiate and compromise so that by the time the message gets to your toddler it is loud and clear, and he knows exactly how to behave. Put yourself in his shoes. If mum leaves him to calm down when he goes into meltdown and dad insists on picking him up as soon as he screams – what is he supposed to think? If mum switches the TV back on if he wails but dad puts the remote in a drawer, he won't know if he's coming or going. He's much more likely to misbehave if he's getting different messages from mum and dad. He may be confused. Or he may be playing one of you against the other. Disagreeing with your partner will only undermine the authority of both of you in the long run.

## Think like a team

If you want to have a brilliantly behaved toddler, mum and dad must develop a consistent 'team' approach. It's important to acknowledge the things that your partner does well as a parent and to learn from them. If you sense an argument is pending about a particular subject, make sure you talk to each other when you are both relaxed, rather than when you are both feeling tired and cranky.

Focus on one issue at a time and keep your eyes on the solution – not the problem. Try asking yourselves, 'How do we want our toddler to behave?' 'What are the different ways we can achieve it?' and 'Which one is likely to work best?' In every instance, try your best to remain calm and listen to what your partner wants to say. Rather than thinking 'I'm right' and 'He (or she) is wrong,' respect your partner's different point of view and be prepared to compromise, negotiate and come up with an action plan that you are both prepared to try. Most of all, agree to be consistent in what you do – you can always review any chosen plan of action if it doesn't seem to be working.

Your toddler learns about life from you. If he sees mum and dad negotiating in a positive way with a little bit of give-and-take on both sides, he will learn to do this too. By working together as a team, you are not only sending a clear message to your toddler about how you want him to behave (which is more likely to result in good behaviour), but you are also teaching him vital life skills.

# What to say and what not to say

The most important thing to avoid is saying opposing things to your toddler and even worse, arguing in front of your toddler. It will undermine the authority of both of you in the long run:

- Don't say: 'I know I'm right and you are wrong.' Do say: 'I understand you have a different opinion on this.'
- Don't say: 'I...' all the time. Do say: 'We...' all the time. The two of you are a team and you need to sort this out together.
- Don't say: 'I'm fed up with always being the bad cop – you never support me.' Do say: 'I would really appreciate it if you can support me when I ask him to do something – let's talk about the best way to get that message across to him.'
- Don't say: 'You do it your way and I'll do it mine and we'll see which works.' Do say: 'We may have different ideas but we have to take the same approach, so let's compromise.'
- Don't say: 'I'm definitely not doing it like that!' Do say: 'Let's both try that for one week and see if it works.'
- Don't say, 'I told you that would work.' Do say: 'Wow! You handled that tantrum brilliantly! Your approach really helped to calm him down.'

## Condensed idea
Sometimes it's healthy to have different ideas, but at other times it's essential for parents to send the same message

# (46) New baby, no problem

When women are pregnant with another child, they often feel excited about the baby but nervous about how their toddler is going to cope. Toddlers can be very demanding at the best of times and may not be thrilled by the idea of sharing mum with a brother or sister.

## Rising to the challenge

If you're pregnant with your second child, you'll probably be asking yourself all sorts of questions. Will I get any sleep? How will I find the time to do everything? How can I feed two hungry mouths at once? How will my toddler cope with all the attention I have to give the baby, when she herself is so clingy at the moment? However, rest assured that mums and dads always rise to a challenge. You will find the time and energy as well as answers to all those questions before very long, provided that you are looking after yourself. It's tempting to wish for super-powers but for now remember you are only human, so make sure you keep yourself as well, as healthy and as energized as you can. Ask your partner, friends and family to help as much as possible with practical support.

## Preparing your toddler

As a mum, you've been through pregnancy before, so you have a good idea of what having a new baby means. However, your toddler has no idea of how family life is about to be turned upside-down. Toddlers have great intuition, so your little one is likely to pick up on how you're feeling. If you're anxious about having two children, she may be too. If you're positive, however, and focus on the exciting things, she will look forward to the new arrival and to having another child to play with.

There are lots of fun things you and your toddler can do to prepare her for the new arrival. Look at pictures together of her when she was a baby and talk about them. Let her choose one of her dolls that is baby-sized and practise handling it gently; perhaps even put a nappy on it together or give the doll a bath. Visit a friend who has a new baby so that your toddler gets an idea of what a real baby is like. Make the idea even more real by letting her choose a baby-grow or a toy to give the new baby on arrival, and painting a picture to put above the baby's cot. By the time the baby arrives, she'll be keen to be your 'special helper'; just make sure she knows that she can help as much or as little as she wants to.

> I think Millie may be busier with her 'new baby' doll than I am with our real new baby! #mumtimes2

## A toddler's view

When a new baby arrives, you should probably get ready for some tantrums and stamping of feet. If this happens, reassure yourself that your toddler's behaviour is absolutely natural (see pages 52–55). Sharing your mum and dad is a challenging concept when you've been used to having them all to yourself. It's a major transition and it takes time – and parental support – to adapt. It's usual for a toddler's behaviour to regress a little while she's getting used to this new state of affairs.

Above all, your toddler needs security and reassurance, because her world has changed dramatically and toddlers dislike changes to their routine. You may be feeling tired, but do what you can to make sure you're giving your toddler attention for the right reasons – not the wrong ones. Notice occasions when she's acting like a particularly good sister and praise her when she does something to show she cares. Be specific about what she is doing well and she'll do it again, so rather than say, 'You are such a lovely sister,' say: 'You are such a lovely sister to hold your brother's hand so gently when you can see he is upset.'

# Introducing a new baby

The very first time your toddler meets her baby brother or sister is a very important occasion, and the days that follow (with a stream of visitors) will have an impact too. Here are a few things for you to bear in mind during those early days:

- Make sure you are with your toddler when she goes to see the baby for the very first time.
- Don't hold the baby in front of you so that he or she forms a 'barrier' between you and your toddler.
- Encourage any visitors to make a fuss of both children.
- Give your toddler lots of kisses and cuddles.
- Explain to her that baby will get presents and she can help unwrap them because baby is too small – and that this is a very special role. Take the chance to show her some of the gifts she received as a baby too.

One important thing to bear in mind: it can be tempting to start saying to your toddler, 'You're a big girl now.' Remember that she may be 'big' compared with your baby – but she is only 'little' really. When you're asking something of her, remember how young she is and make sure it's a realistic request.

## One-to-one time with your toddler

As all parents with a new baby will know, there is a lot to do and never enough time to do it. But it is important for your toddler that you both create some special time with her, when the baby is not around demanding your attention. Giving her one-to-one time will send her a

clear message that she is precious and not second in your priorities. This helps avoid feelings of sibling rivalry (see pages 55–55). Make sure she knows you love her as much as you have always done by creating special time together each day that is baby-free (unless your toddler brings baby into the chat). As well as one-to-one time with mum and dad, arrange for her to have special time with other family members. This will be beneficial for her and for them, and it will give you some time off.

Also, remember to show her that there are distinct benefits to being a toddler instead of a baby. There are things she can do with you that baby cannot – like wrapping your arms around each other, sharing a book together or doing a jigsaw or painting.

## Condensed idea
### Help your toddler to become positive about a new baby by providing lots of love and reassurance

# 47 From ideal to real

Everyone has an opinion on the best way to parent toddlers – even people without children – but your toddler and your relationship with him is unique. That makes you the expert. While you may value the views of others, it's important to develop your own style.

## Am I doing okay?

Being a mum or dad is the most important job we'll ever do in our lives and yet we have no real preparation for it. We take lessons to learn how to drive or swim, but when it comes to being a parent, we're somehow assumed to be 'naturally' good at it. But being a mum or dad is a steep learning curve – it goes pretty much straight up!

Every mum and dad wonders if they are dealing with their toddler in the 'right way', so rest assured that if you do ask yourself this from time to time, it's normal. You're investing time and energy in being the parent you want to be. You're in a lifelong relationship with your child, and probably feel that your parenting skills will affect who he is as he grows older – this puts you under considerable pressure. The first priority is to check that you're not ignoring the thing you do well, and only focusing on the things you're struggling to cope with. This is natural when it seems that no sooner have you cracked one toddler-challenge than another rears its head. To make it harder, what works for one of your children may not work for another. You may have one child who drops off to sleep without a murmur and another who gets a fresh injection of energy come bedtime. You are the same parent, but each one of your children is different and so you will need to adapt your parenting style to respond to each of them.

# Trial and error

When it comes to raising a toddler, there is no magic formula that works for everyone. Being a mum or dad is about daily trial and error, and as your children grow, you'll find you acquire lots of tools in your toolbox to deal with different situations. If you sense trouble brewing, ask yourself, 'How do I want my toddler to behave?', 'What can I do to help him get to that point?' and 'What messages is he sending me that I need to hear?' Sometimes you won't be sure, so you'll try something that you hope will help. If it works, that's great, but if it doesn't, don't take that to mean that you have 'failed' – it simply means that it's time to try something else. However, make sure you give your strategies a good amount of time: toddlers need at least a week to get used to things.

## You can do it!

The key to achieving your potential as a parent is to believe in yourself. If you want to do it, you will. Here are some ideas to help you:

- Always listen to your 'gut instinct' – this has been shown to be based upon experience, knowledge and an assessment of the current situation.
- Listen to the advice of people you trust, but ultimately make your own decisions.
- Do what you want to do, not what other people tell you to do.
- Acknowledge that you are the expert on your child. And believe it.
- Focus on what you think, not what other people think.
- If you try something and it works, do it again.
- If you try something and it doesn't work, try something else.

# Have a plan ready

There are likely to be times when you are surrounded by people who have very strong opinions about how you should and shouldn't parent your toddler. This happens to everyone and you can feel especially in the spotlight if your little one goes into meltdown in front of an audience. This is the very time that it's important to be the parent you want to be. It's not going to be easy, and in fact, you need to acknowledge that this is a real challenge – everyone finds it hard to be the mum or dad they want to be when they are surrounded by lots of people with different ideas.

It can be particularly challenging if it's your mother-in-law – and your partner insists on sitting on the fence. Plan now what you intend to do if your toddler does have a very public meltdown (see page 71), so that you already know how you will deal with it.

# Dealing with unwanted advice

Begin by recognizing that other people are probably offering advice because they want to help. They may even be saying some things that are useful, even if not all of them are. If the other person is a member of

the family, the reason that you both have strong opinions is because you both want what is best for your toddler, so remember that, essentially, you're on the same side! Try to be positive in the way you deal with the other person, even if they appear to be quite critical (they might not actually mean to be critical) and you are feeling defensive. Tell them what you appreciate about their support (hopefully there will be something!), be clear and confident about what you are doing, and carry on doing it.

> Instruction booklet for toddler seems to have been lost in post. #whatnow?

You don't have to justify yourself or go into chapter and verse about your approach to prove that it's better than theirs. Just do what you want to do and what you feel is right. If it helps, identify the times that are likely to be stressful and confrontational with your toddler, like mealtimes or bedtimes, and make sure there is no one else around at that time. Instead, welcome other people into your home at times that suit you, when you feel more relaxed and confident.

## Be a great role model

As a parent, you will want your child to grow up being an independent and confident person, who seeks advice from people whose opinions he values, but who makes his own decisions about his life. We all want our children to be their own person and not to grow up living a life that other people tell him to live. So as you deal with other people's suggestions and advice, now is a good time to set that great example, by being the parent you want to be.

## Condensed idea
### Be the parent you want to be, not the parent others want you to be

# Dealing with tension

Arguments between parents are a normal part of family life. They are also opportunities to teach your toddler how to handle disagreements positively and the benefits of being able to compromise. Here are some tips for handling arguments in front of your toddler.

## You're the role model

Disagreements between family members are inevitable. Sometimes there will be arguments about the small things, like whose turn it is to empty the dishwasher, and sometimes it will be about much bigger issues. However, if you both treat each other with respect, listen to what each wants to say and are willing to negotiate and resolve the conflict in a positive way, it can actually be a good thing for your toddler to witness. You're both providing great role models for her and when she comes up against conflict in her own life, she'll probably try out some of the strategies you've demonstrated.

> Being a parent seems to be improving my negotiating skills. Who knew? #talkingitover

On the other hand, arguments in which you don't show respect for each other, or listen to each other, will have a negative impact. We've all experienced arguments like this. It's hard to be calm and reasonable when you are feeling annoyed and stressed, and when arguments become very heated, we may end up saying things we later regret. But when arguing with your partner, it's worth remembering that if you shout and stamp your feet to make yourself heard, that's exactly what your toddler will do.

## Be honest

Witnessing tension between mum and dad is upsetting for a toddler.
Even if she doesn't understand every word, she knows what's happening.
She may feel frightened and it's normal for toddlers to believe they are
the cause of the argument (because they still see themselves as the centre
of the world). In this kind of situation, a toddler needs reassurance. If you
and your partner argue in front of your toddler, be honest about it; don't
pretend that nothing has happened. Talk to her together, reassure her
and tell her that you love her. Say sorry to each other and let her know
you are going to try harder to talk to each other instead of shouting.

## Dealing with separation

If tension in your family leads to separation or divorce, it's likely to be
a very tough time for both parents and children. It may be one of the
hardest challenges you face as a parent – to break the news to your
toddler that mum and dad are no longer going to live together. When

# If you decide to separate

The way you and your partner communicate with each other and with your toddler during a separation will be key to the way she copes with the major transition. Here are some ideas to help:

- Keep as many aspects of your toddler's routine as consistent as possible so that she continues to feel secure.
- Keep reassuring her that you both love her very much.
- If you do argue, imagine that there is a friend in the room with you who is watching what's going on. It may help you act more calmly and reasonably.
- Take 'time out'. Rather than try to talk during the heat of the moment, set up a time to talk about it when you are both feeling more in control.
- If your toddler is more demanding than usual, understand why this may be happening but keep your boundaries in place. She will feel more secure if she knows these exist and don't change.
- Sort out times for each of you to spend with your toddler.
- Avoid the 'blame game'. She doesn't need to know the details. She needs to know that mum and dad still love her.
- Avoid talking about the separation or divorce to friends and family in front of your toddler.
- Keep talking to your toddler and answering her questions. Reading books can help. Let her know it's okay to talk about her feelings.
- Keep as positive as you can. Your love for your toddler and hers for you will help you through this difficult time.

you are struggling to cope with lots of emotions and practical challenges yourself, it can be really hard to handle the situation positively so that your toddler doesn't suffer.

Remember that toddlers find any kind of change frightening. Your toddler's behaviour may regress: she may be more demanding than usual and throw more tantrums, and she may find it more difficult to sleep, or lose her appetite. She may develop fears about things she is not normally afraid of. That's natural. It's because she is feeling insecure and she needs time to come to terms with what's going on in her little life.

## Talk to her together

You may have got to the point where you and your partner seem to disagree on everything but there is one thing you must agree on: to both behave in a way that will help your toddler deal with this. Talk to her together and keep your words simple and clear. Your toddler thinks the universe revolves around her, so explain it in terms of the practical impact it will have on her. Use language she will understand, such as: 'We both love you very much and always will... mum and dad are going to live in different houses and you will spend time with each of us... we will both see you and have fun with you.' Be sure to talk to her when you both have lots of time, so you can give her lots of cuddles and kisses, not when she's just about to go to bed and will be on her own.

Your toddler needs to know she is going to be loved by both of you, and this will not change. In the midst of an upheaval, give her that very important message to hold on to. During a separation, toddlers need lots of reassurance and consistency of behaviour from both parents.

## Condensed idea
### Arguments happen – but handled well, they can be a positive learning experience

# 49 Blended families

If you're no longer with your toddler's father or mother, and have now met someone else with whom to have a serious relationship, you'll want your toddler to meet them. This chapter looks at managing this in a way that keeps everyone happy.

## One step at a time

Your toddler's first meeting with your new partner is a big and important step for all of you, so you need to do it at a time that feels right. Don't feel obliged to 'get it over and done with' in a hurry; take your time and sense when everyone feels ready to do this. Forming a relationship with a new partner creates all kinds of challenges, and this meeting will be the first of many, so it needs to be approached very positively. View this as a new and exciting chapter for all of you. Think about ways to take this one step at a time; your toddler will find the idea easier if he meets your partner first, then his or her family at a later date. It's also a good idea to make the first meeting somewhere neutral and away from home – somewhere you know your child will be excited about going to. Introduce your partner as a friend and do something you can all have fun doing together, such as playing football in the park and having a picnic.

The first time your toddler meets your new partner, make sure you give him lots of time and cuddles afterwards, and talk to him about what you've both enjoyed during your day all together. Also talk to your new partner about what he or she is feeling and what you can both do to help and support each other, particularly as both of you are likely to be feeling anxious. As time goes on, encourage your partner to get more and more involved in different aspects of daily life, such as mealtimes and bedtime

# Top tips to help the transition

When families merge, your toddler will really need the adults to present a united front. Here are some tips to help you and your new partner become part of a team:

- Give children plenty of reassurance and security.
- Be fair to all children and consistent in the way you manage their behaviour.
- Initially, take the lead in managing your toddler's behaviour (with support from your new partner).
- Praise children for behaving well with their step-siblings.
- Talk to your new partner about how he or she can support you.
- Spend time with your toddler on his own so that he feels reassured and knows how important he is in your life.
- Stick to boundaries. Don't relax them just because you may be feeling guilty about the breakdown of your relationship.
- Maintain a good relationship with the person you've separated from. Let your toddler see the two of you working together.

routines. It's very important that you take it slowly and gently so that your toddler can gradually get used to the changes he's experiencing. It will also help you and your partner adjust to forming a new family.

## Listen to the children

Being a step-mum or step-dad can be tough as you all become used to living together and getting along as one extended family. It's a time of great change, and in addition, you and your partner may have different ideas on how children should be brought up – you have different family rules. New relationships and a newly blended family mean that everyone has to invest time, energy and commitment in making it work. Acknowledge what is going well and talk about what you want to change, so that you can agree a strategy together as circumstances change along the way. If you do have different ideas about certain family issues, resolve them through talking, well away from little ears.

When children in the blended family behave in a challenging way, try to understand the situation from their perspective. Don't be too quick to think you know what they mean or are doing; reflect carefully on the messages being sent by all the members of your blended family. The children will be getting used to a new situation and you need to acknowledge that, but at the same time, it is vital to keep long-standing boundaries in place. These are more important than ever at a time of big change in your toddler's life.

# It's not personal

Toddlers don't like changes to their routine, no matter how small. So introducing a new person into family life can often affect their behaviour. It would be quite natural for your toddler to stamp his feet and have a tantrum and to be generally more demanding than usual when two families join together. Don't take it personally, and reassure your new partner not to take it personally either. Your toddler's behaviour

> Now five children, three cats and one dog. Not sure which is trickiest. #expandedfamily

will be an indication of what he's going through and how he's trying to cope with a new and different situation. If both of you recognize this and understand what lies behind any changes in behaviour, you will both be much better equipped to deal with it.

The most important thing is that you and your new partner keep working to build a sense of connection between him or her and your

toddler. That sense of connection may come quickly or it may take time, but bear in mind that every situation and every relationship is different. If your toddler refuses to play ball, keep working at it; you will get there in the end. You may need to be very patient, as when two families blend together, everyone needs time to get used to it – both children and adults. It's also common for toddlers to see the new adult partner as a competitor for their parent's attention. But as your toddler gets to know your partner better, and to adjust to what's going on, he's likely to develop a new and special relationship with that key person. In many ways, toddlers find it easier to handle mum or dad's new relationship than teenagers do. This is because toddlers like close family relationships – they want them to work. However, you can't force it, so let it happen at its own speed. Give your toddler time and you'll be surprised at the strength of the relationships he can build with step-parents and siblings.

# Condensed idea
## Step-families take time to build, so don't expect perfect behaviour from day one

# 50 Parents are pioneers

When a child is born, a mum and dad are born too, and an adventure begins. As a parent, you are a pioneer exploring uncharted territory on a daily basis. It's a white-knuckle rollercoaster ride: exciting, challenging and exhilarating, with huge ups and downs.

## Creative parenting

This book has suggested lots of practical ideas and strategies for helping you to get on well with and to understand the behaviour of your toddler, no matter what circumstances arise. You've learned that you are a toddler's most important role model, and that what you say and do has a much bigger influence on toddler behaviour than anything else. The very fact that you decided to read this book puts you ahead of the game, because it means that you're already focusing on the right person – your toddler. Along with accepting this responsibility comes the understanding of how it is that you come to be the expert on your child, what works for your family and how you're at the heart of it. You know your toddler, you know yourself, and you can take all the tips we've given you to create a toolbox that's all your own. Parents are fantastic problem-solvers who come up with inventive solutions on a daily basis.

A parent's responsibility can seem overwhelming, but it also means that every day you have the opportunity to have a positive impact on your toddler's life. Everything you do and say as a parent affects not only her behaviour, but her relationship skills and the person she will grow up to be. It's always a two-way thing: while putting into practice some of the ideas in this book, you'll not only have been developing your own skills as a parent, but helping your toddler to develop her skills too. The way you respond to your toddler will help in building her confidence, giving her self-belief and establishing positive values, skills and qualities in her that she will carry all through her life. Your toddler is like a blank canvas and you are the passionate and talented artist with the skills and the tools to create a masterpiece. As a mum or dad, you add colour, vibrancy, depth and meaning to the life of your child on a daily basis: values that are priceless. And, as a result, she is the sum of all the time and energy you invest in her as well as the love you give her.

## You're at the helm

The key thing to remember as a mum or dad is that if there is something you want to change – you're the one who is in charge of making that change. Having a positive impact on a toddler's behaviour comes down to understanding what might be causing that particular behaviour and then making changes to the way that you behave – in the way that you respond to her. If it feels as though you're a pioneer on a steep learning curve, think about how it looks to your toddler! She's a pioneer too, trying to find ways to cope with a whole range of new feelings and experiences. So don't desert her in her tantrumming hour of need; step up to the plate, put aside your frustration and any preconceived ideas, and really listen. Then act accordingly, taking all things into consideration. If at any time you feel that your toddler seems to be somehow in charge, commit to climbing back into the driving seat and take control. If you believe you can do it – you will.

# Top parenting tips

Family life is a work in progress. Make a difference by taking one step at a time in a new direction, and you will keep moving forwards. Here are some top tips – but remember that your ideas will always be better than ours, because your family is unique and you know it better than anyone:

- Be the mum or dad you want to be – not the one your toddler 'makes you' become.
- Go with your gut instinct – it will be spot on.
- Enjoy being an 'imperfect' parent with an 'imperfect' toddler – that's what makes family life fun.
- Step into your toddler's shoes and see the world through her eyes. Tune into the messages she's sending you and what's making her behave in the way that she is.
- Give your toddler attention for the right reasons – not the wrong ones. Behaviour that gets attention is repeated.
- Remember your A–B–C: Always Be Consistent.
- Always act your age, not your toddler's.
- The adult your child will become is not defined by academic success. People are shaped by all the cuddles, laughs and challenges they shared as a child.
- Take time to celebrate your achievements as a parent.
- Look after yourself – and have the energy to be the best mum or dad you can be.
- Don't beat yourself up about the mistakes you've made as a parent; concentrate on the things you succeed at.
- Tell your toddler you love them, often.

# Look to the future

It may seem like an impossibly long way off, but stop for a few minutes to think about yourself when your children are fully grown and have toddlers of their own. Close your eyes and picture yourself surrounded by the people you love and imagine how it will feel. What would you like your son or daughter to say they love the most about you as a mum or dad? How would you like to hear them describing you to their own children? That's the person you are now. If you could pass on one piece of advice to your child about being a mum or a dad, what would that one nugget be? Write it down – and then take your own advice.

Today is the first day of the rest of your life. You are in control of your life as it moves forwards, so make your world a great place to be. Don't look back with any regrets. You can't change the past, but you can create your future, so look forward to what lies ahead and the fun you're going to have

> Today like skiing down a black run. Fast, exciting, but pretty terrifying. All survived! #pioneerfamily

with your children. The time you have with them is precious, so make family life a fun and daring adventure. Don't expect to cruise along without difficulties or challenges, but do commit to rising to them. Be a pioneer – and raise a pioneer. Your son or daughter will always follow in your footsteps so the more you take responsibility for your life and enjoy the adventure, the more easily your children will be able to meet every challenge with good humour and impeccable behaviour.

## Condensed idea
### Be a pioneer parent who teaches a toddler not only how to behave, but how to live

# Index

# Acknowledgements

**Author acknowledgements**

With thanks to the special people who have made my book possible.

The team at Quercus for commissioning a book I have had so much fun writing. My editor Sarah for her energy, enthusiasm, vision and expertise. Tracy for her fabulous and innovative design work. Alice for her editing. Tim for being a real blessing in my life. Roy, Ken, Keith and everyone in my family for their love and support. Sarah, Gill, Tree, Elaine and Megumi for always being there for me. Mum and dad for always believing in me. Josh and Holly for all of their love and laughter and for making me the happiest mum in the world. Ben for being awesome. Jerry for encouraging me to be my own person and for his love and support at every step of my journey.

And all of the parents I have had the privilege to coach.


**Picture credits**

Incidental images used throughout.
**Fotolia:** Agence Design; Alfaolga; Andrey7777777; Daganm; Didem Hizar; Ilyaka; Khorzhevska; Leremy; HuHu Lin; Log88off; Pavel Losevsky; Oksun70; Alexander Potapov; Zodiaribi
**Shutterstock:** W. Jarva; Osijan
**iStockphoto:** Bubaone

Quercus Publishing Plc
55 Baker Street, 7th Floor,
South Block, London W1U 8EW

First published in 2013

Copyright © Quercus 2013

A catalogue record of this book is available from the British Library

ISBN 978 1 78206 138 0
Printed and bound in China

10 9 8 7 6 5 4 3 2 1

Produced for Quercus Publishing Plc by
Tracy Killick Art Direction and Design

**Commissioning editor:** Sarah Tomley
(of www.editorsonline.org)
**Designer:** Tracy Killick
**Project editor:** Alice Bowden
**Proof-reader:** Louise Abbott
**Illustrator:** Victoria Woodgate
(www.vickywoodgate.com)
**Indexer:** Hilary Bird